Chuck and Blanche J

Savor Montana™ Cookbook

Chuck J.
Enjoy!
Blanche Johnson

Montana's Finest Restaurants & Lodges
Their Recipes & Their Histories

Wilderness Adventures Press, Inc.™
Belgrade, Montana

This book was manufactured with an easy-open, lay-flat binding.

Maps, book design, and cover design © 2003 Wilderness Adventures Press, Inc.™

Published by Wilderness Adventures Press, Inc.™
45 Buckskin Road
Belgrade, MT 59714
1-800-925-3339
Website: www.wildadv.com
Email: books@wildadv.com

First Edition
10 9 8 7 6 5 4 3 2 1

Printed in the United States of America

Library of Congress Cataloging-in-Publication Data

Johnson, Chuck.
  Savor Montana cookbook : Montana's finest restaurants, their recipes and their histories / by Chuck Johnson and Blanche Johnson.– 1st American pbk. ed.
      p. cm.
  ISBN 1-932098-04-6 (alk. paper)
  1. Restaurants–Montana–Guidebooks. 2. Cookery–Montana. I. Johnson, Blanche, 1943- II. Title.
  TX907.3.M85J64 2003
  647.95786–dc21

                                                                        2003013059

TABLE OF CONTENTS

—Cascade—

Table of Contents

Fishing on the Gallatin River at the turn of the century was not so different from today. One still must keep a watchful eye for the occasional grizzly.

INTRODUCTION

When Blanche and I first started spending time in Montana we were pleasantly surprised at the quality of the many restaurants around the state. Many great chefs moved to Big Sky Country to get out of the hectic lifestyle of the big cities, bringing their culinary skills with them.

We decided to feature some of these fine restaurants in the first title in our cookbook series: *Savor Montana*. Many of these establishments also have lodging, fishing, skiing, and other outdoor activities. Take a trip through Montana and enjoy our gourmet restaurants and take this cookbook back home with you.

We hope you enjoy your travels here as much as John Steinbeck did when he penned the following lines in his famous book, *Travels with Charley*, "I am in love with Montana. For other states I have admiration, respect, recognition, even some affection, but with Montana it is love."

*Some of Montana's remote dude ranches had to pack in
all of the supplies for guests.*

ACKNOWLEDGMENTS

We would like to give our special thanks to the owners, managers, and chefs of the featured restaurants for their help in gathering the information for this book, as well as their generosity in sharing some of their favorite recipes with us.

We also want to give recognition to our graphic designer, Marcia Rueter Leritz, for her effort in getting this project to fruition, and for her graphic skills and many of the photographs used in the design of this book.

Savor Montana™ Cookbook

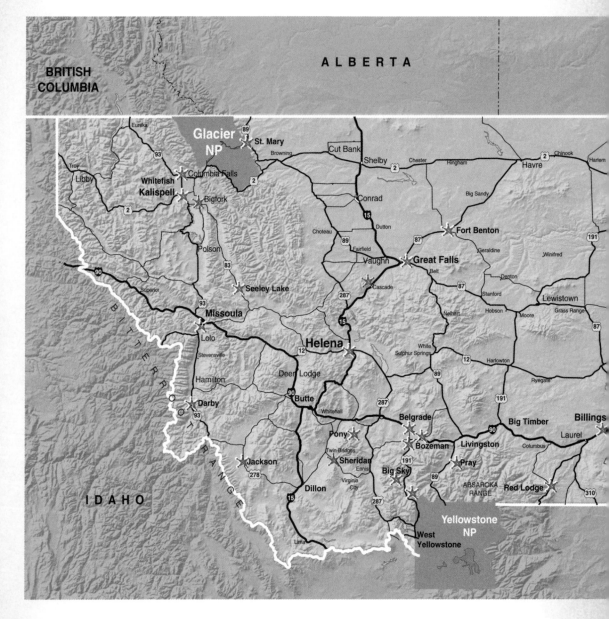

0   100 Miles

0   100KM

⭐ **Restaurant Locations**

RESTAURANTS FEATURED

SASKATCHEWAN

Opheim   Outlook   Westby
Flaxville
Scobey   Plentywood
Medicine Lake
Saco   Froid
Malta   Nashua   Wolf Point   Poplar   Brockton   Culbertson
Glasgow
Fairview
Richey   Sidney
Jordan   Circle
Glendive
MONTANA   Wibaux
Terry
Melstone   12   Ismay
Hysham   Miles City   Plevna
Forsyth   Baker
Hardin   Colstrip   Ekalaka
Broadus
Lodge Grass   90   212

WYOMING

MONTANA FACTS

Fourth largest state in the union

    147,138 square miles

    93,157,953 acres

    550 miles east to west

    275 miles north to south

Elevations - 1,820 feet to 12,798 feet

Counties - 56

Towns and Cities - 126

Population (2000 census) - 902,195

    7 Indian Reservations

    2 National Parks

    11 National Forests

    68 State Recreation Areas

    12 Wilderness Areas

    11 State Parks

Nicknames

    Treasure State

    Big Sky Country

    Land of the Shining Mountains

Food tastes and trends have changed in Montana since the turn of the century, but the spectacular landscapes haven't.

Primary Industries

    Agriculture

    Timber

    Mining

    Tourism

Bitterroot lewisia.

Capital - Helena

Bird - Western Meadowlark

Animal - Grizzly Bear

Flower - Bitterroot

Fish - Black-spotted Cutthroat

Tree - Ponderosa Pine

Gemstone - Montana Agate

Grass - Bluebunch Wheatgrass

For free travel information on Montana, see: www.visitmt.com or call 1-800-VISIT MT (1-800-847-4868) or 406-841-2870.

Enzo
Mediterranean
Bistro

Established 1998

1502 Rehberg Lane
Billings, Montana

Reservations recommended
406-651-0999

Lunch 11:30 am to 2:00 pm
(Tuesday thru Friday)

Dinner nightly at 5:00 pm

Enzo Mediterranean Bistro

James Honaker, Owner
Laurent Zirotti, General Manager

Over time, on its way to the Missouri, the Yellowstone River cut deep into the earth, creating the present-day Yellowstone Valley. This action exposed the magnificent sandstone cliffs that are today a Billings landmark. From the valley floor near the river, it's over 460 feet to the top of the rimrocks. Buffalo and other wildlife flourished along this broad valley and the adjacent plains during the early 19th century and served as a lifeline for Native Americans.

Even before Montana became a state in November of 1889, Billings was starting to prosper. The Minnesota and Montana Land and Improvement Company purchased Northern Pacific grant lands in the Billings area in 1882, which included land for forty miles on either side of the railroad tracks in that area. Up until that time, there were only three buildings on the site now known as Billings—a large wooden structure on Montana Avenue, which housed railroad engineers and supervisors, a store on Minnesota Avenue and a home on 27th Street. By the fall of that same year, 155 businesses, 99 homes, 6 railroad buildings, and a church were kicking off Billings's boom.

Today, Billings is the largest city in Montana and functions as the hub for a region larger than 125,000 square miles, and it remains a highly productive agricultural region for crops and cattle.

The Enzo Mediterranean Bistro is a relatively recent addition to the Billings culinary scene, but it has quickly gained a reputation as one of the best restaurants in the region.

It is a new building influenced by the Tuscan/Provence farmhouse architectural style. The varied menu includes a taste of the Mediterranean in addition to classic American dishes that include Montana's fine beef along with fresh fish arriving from both coasts. There is a fine selection of wines and beers to complement your meal.

General Manager Laurent Zirotti grew up in France. After meeting James Honaker in San Francisco, Laurent and his family moved to the Billings area to open and manage Enzo.

MUSSELS MARINIÈRE
Appetizer

Ingredients

5	pounds mussels (Penn Cove in USA)
1	ounce unsweetened butter
¼	liter dry white wine
6	each shallots
	Salt and pepper

2   ounces butter

1   ounce fresh parsley

OPTIONAL INGREDIENTS

Artichoke hearts, cooked

Roma tomatoes, diced

Preparation

WASH the mussels thoroughly.

IN A SAUCEPAN, combine mussels, white wine, diced shallots, salt, pepper, and half the chopped parsley (add artichokes and tomatoes at this point if you want). Cook over medium fire with a lid. Mussels are cooked when they open up. Do not serve mussels that do not open (discard). Put mussels in a serving dish and reduce the sauce to one-third. When sauce is ready, stop the fire and add the butter to the sauce with a whip (whisk). Add parsley to taste for seasoning and pour over mussels.

SPRINKLE the other half of parsley over dish.

Serves 8

SAUTÉED STUFFED SALMON
with Smoked Salmon—served with Citrus Salsa

For the Salmon

4	thick pieces of filet fresh salmon		Panko bread crumbs, preferably
4	thin slices of smoked salmon		Oil and butter
	Basil pesto		

Preparation

BUTTERFLY each filet of fresh salmon (skin off). Spread filet with a tablespoon of basil pesto and lay a piece of smoked salmon in between, then fold back together. Bread lightly and sauté in a pan with butter and oil. Cook the salmon until brown on both sides and finish in oven until pink in the middle.

For the Citrus Salsa

1	orange cut into segments	½	Bermuda onion, chopped finely
2	tomatoes, diced	2	tablespoons of rice wine vinegar
2	scallions, diced	3	tablespoons of olive oil
1	garlic clove, chopped finely		Salt and pepper to taste
5	leaves of basil, chopped		

Preparation

COMBINE all prepared vegetables together, add vinegar, and while stirring, slowly add the olive oil.

SERVE cooked salmon over steamed rice and spoon Citrus Salsa on top.

Serves 4

FROZEN ITALIAN BITTERSWEET CHOCOLATE GELATO

Ingredients

9 ounces bittersweet chocolate
   (best quality available)

⅔ cup heavy cream brought to a boil

7 egg yolks

1 ⅛ cups sugar (10 ounces)

2 cups heavy cream, whipped

2 ounces liqueur of your choice,
   such as Amaretto or Frangelica

Preparation

CHOP chocolate and melt over water bath. Whip yolks and sugar to ribbon stage. Add melted chocolate to ribboned yolks, then mix in hot cream. Add liqueur. Fold in whipped cream. Freeze in container and scoop, or freeze in individual molds.

TOP with an espresso whipped cream, powdered sugar, and powdered cocoa or other garnishes of your choice.

Serves 8

One of the early-day Missouri River steamboats, "The Montana."

*Summer attracts crowds of cowboys, cowgirls, and onlookers to Billings
and other communities, large and small, throughout Montana.*

Walkers Grill

WALKERS GRILL

Established 1993

301 N. 27th Street
Billings, Montana
406-245-9291

**Located in the lower level of
the historic Chamber Building**

Reservations recommended
**Dinner, Monday – Saturday
5:30 to 10:30 (Closed Sunday)**

**Live jazz Friday and Saturday
8:00 to 10:30 pm**

Walkers Grill

Bill Honaker, Owner
Jeremy Bernhard, Chef

Bill Honaker at Walkers Grill.

This restaurant has been honored by the *Wine Spectator* for having one of the most outstanding restaurant wine lists in the world. The historic Chamber of Commerce building endures in the new life given it by this lively bistro and dinner house. The original kitchen has been opened up and the wood paneling has a new light stain, but in the back room everything is exactly as it has been since 1910.

Walkers is a 132-seat, full-service restaurant with a full bar—a well-established local favorite and a destination for travelers, theater-goers, and museum patrons alike. Menu selections offer freshness and simplicity while the professional waitstaff contribute friendly service in a casual, yet urban, dining setting. Walkers opened its doors in February of 1993 and has collected critical acclaim ever since. It has been a recipient of the Award of Excellence by *Wine Spectator* for several years, as well as receiving write-ups in the *Wall Street Journal*, *Billings Gazette*, *Frommer's Guide*, and *Montana Magazine*. It has served such noted guests as Mel Gibson, Lou Gosset, Jr., Jon Voight, Garrison Keillor, Joan Baez, Poet Alan Ginsberg, and most notably, President Bill Clinton.

James and Bill Honaker and Michael Callaghan originally opened the restaurant, but James has since left to open Enzo, a Mediterranean eatery also featured in this publication, and Michael Callaghan has left to be a restaurant consultant at FSA.

Current owner Bill Honaker continues the Walkers tradition of excellence in food, wine, and service.

"Old wine to drink, old friends to trust."

Bourbon Street Pasta

Ingredients

1	pound andouille sausage, cut into half-moons
2	red bell peppers, diced large
1	green bell peppers, diced large
1	yellow onion, chopped
1	rib celery, diced fine
½-2	(depending on strength of peppers) Scotch bonnet peppers, minced
¼	head fresh garlic, minced
	Olive oil

IN LARGE stockpot, sauté sausage in a small amount of oil. Add vegetables, Scotch bonnets, and garlic. Stirring often, continue cooking until peppers become slightly tender.

Add

1	cup (plus) tomato stricia*
½	tablespoon ground cumin
¼	teaspoon celery salt
3	teaspoons gumbo filé
½	teaspoon cayenne pepper
⅛	cup Worcestershire sauce
1 ⅓	cups white wine

STIR and allow to simmer about 5 minutes.

Then add

10	ounces beef broth
10	ounces chicken broth
	Salt and pepper to taste
	Minced cilantro

BRING to a boil; add minced cilantro after cooling.

TOSS with cooked penne or linguini pasta.

Serves 8

Tomato stricia is a canned product (available from Sysco) of California ripened tomato strips packed in tomato purée. Can substitue other canned tomato purée.

DUCK SAUCE MARIONBERRY

Ingredients

1 pound marionberries	1 cup sherry vinegar
4 tablespoons ginger, minced	1 cup sugar
4 tablespoons shallots, minced	1 can chicken broth

BRING everything but the chicken broth to boil. Reduce till very syrupy. Add broth. Bring to a boil. Thicken with cornstarch if desired. Adjust seasonings. Run through finest blade on food mill.

MAKES enough sauce for four duck breasts.

Duck Breasts

4 duck breasts   *Olive oil*

IN SAUTÉ pan, add 1 tablespoon olive oil, bring to high heat. Sear duck breasts, both sides, fatty side first, to medium rare. Let rest for 5 minutes. Slice and plate. Drizzle Duck Sauce Marionberry over slices.

Serves 4

Walkers Bar is a popular spot for friends to meet in Billings.

WALKERS APPLE CRISP

Topping

½	cup brown sugar
1	cup flour
½	teaspoon cinnamon

½	teaspoon salt
¼	cup butter (softened) cut into small squares

Preparation

COMBINE in mixer with paddle, medium speed.

MIX until topping breaks into small crumbles.

Apple Crisp

4-6	Granny Smith apples, peeled and sliced

¼	cup lemon (juice)
¾	cup sugar

Preparation

PREHEAT oven to 350°F.

PRESS apples evenly into a 9 x 12-inch (4-inch deep) baking dish. Add topping; pack loosely. Bake at 350°F, 45 minutes to 1 hour.

The Bridger Mountains north of Bozeman.

The Pollard Hotel

Established 1893

2 North Broadway
Red Lodge, Montana

Dining—5:30 to 9:30 pm
Sunday Brunch—9:00 am
to 1:00 pm

Reservations recommended
406-446-0001 or 1-800-POLLARD
www.pollardhotel.com
pollard@pollardhotel.com

The Pollard Hotel

Sharon Nix, Proprietor
Rusty Olson, Chef

*C*ertainly a great deal of excitement must have been gener-ated with the building of the first brick structure in Red Lodge in 1893. The Spofford Hotel was built at the point midway between the train passenger depot and the thickly settled portion of the city. Thomas F. Pollard took possession of the thir-ty-five-room hotel in 1902, renaming it "The Pollard" and adding twenty-five rooms. The dining room was a lovely room in the early days, with fine furnishings, high quality hotel linens, dishes, silverware, and glassware. In the early days the hotel was noted for its excellent cuisine and specialized in broiled lobsters and other dishes suitable even to the most particular gourmets. This famous hotel has been the gathering place of political, the-atrical, and many celebrated personalities. Names such as William Jennings Bryan, the famed silver-tongued orator; General Miles, the Indian Fighter; and the copper kings, William and Marcus Daly, dotted the early hotel register. Buffalo Bill Cody spent many an evening in the lobby swapping tales with local old timers. Calamity Jane would on occasion interrupt the quietness of this old lodging place, and the noted Indian scout Liver Eatin' Johnston who lived here in the early days, occasionally frequented the establishment.

- Barbara Pollard Sanford

*T*he Pollard was originally, and is still today, the cornerstone of Red Lodge and a center for warm hospitality. Since the Pollard family last owned the hotel, it has been vari-ously known as The Chief, The Tyler, and The Cielo Grande. Mr. Fred Mackaman, who bought the hotel and renamed it The Cielo Grande, had grand ideas for the hotel, including a swimming pool, miniature golf course, and accommodations for 90 to 114 guests. Unfortunately, the ideas for the hotel were much grander than Mr. Mackaman's wallet, and he was unable to complete his vision. The hotel fell into disuse for many years.

In September of 1991, the Hotel Company of Red Lodge purchased The Pollard with the intention of making it one of the finest small hotels in the Rocky Mountain West. The build-ing was fully restored creating a hotel that embraced its colorful history while maintaining modern comforts. All of the exterior rooms were dismantled, and the windows, ceilings, car-pets, furniture, draperies, and linens were replaced.

Beginning in the fall of 1992, work was begun on the new interior guest rooms and the building of The Gallery and the History Room. Both The Gallery, with its coffered ceilings and fireplace, and The History Room, a comfortable room with information chronicling the

Three generations of Pollards.

history of the area and hotel, were designed to reflect the philosophy of warm, western hospitality.

The dining room and kitchen were created from what had been office space and a barbershop. Elements of the original lobby have been kept intact and contribute to the welcome extended to guests. The restaurant merges the relaxing atmosphere of the West with carefully prepared selections from the chef.

A number of activities are easily accessible to those who pass through Red Lodge, Montana. Residing at the base of the Beartooth Highway and Chief Joseph Highway, two of Montana's most scenic byways, Red Lodge is an idyllic Montana town. The great outdoors is at one's fingertips in Red Lodge, with fly fishing, hiking, backpacking, biking, hunting, picnicking, whitewater rafting, snow-shoeing, cross-country skiing (Red Lodge Nordic Center) and down-hill skiing (Red Lodge Mountain). Yellowstone and Grand Teton National Parks are an easy drive and worth a visit. For the historian, the Buffalo Bill Historical Center, Little Bighorn Battlefield, and the Carbon County Peaks to Plains Museum of History are all close enough for a visit.

Red Lodge also has a number of local traditions such as their annual rodeo, the Fourth of July parade, and the infamous Pig Races every Friday, Saturday, and Sunday night during the summer months,

Each year at the beginning of August, Red Lodge hosts the Festival of Nations, celebrating the early mining history of a town peopled by different ethnic groups—Italians, Finns, Scots, Germans, and Slavs. This festival of food, song, and folkways draws thousands of visitors and locals yearly.

The Pollard's restored lobby.

Hotel guests on the porch in 1896.

15

STUFFED PORTABELLA MUSHROOMS

Ingredients

16 ounces cream cheese	Salt and pepper to taste
1 cup sundried tomatoes	Fresh Parmesan cheese
1 cup spinach, chopped and blanched	Fresh portabella mushrooms
1 tablespoon fresh garlic, chopped	Balsamic vinegar, reduced
1 teaspoon onion powder	

Preparation

PREHEAT oven to 375°F.

COMBINE all ingredients excluding mushrooms and Parmesan. Remove gills from mushrooms with a spoon. Stuff mushrooms with cream cheese mixture and top with fresh grated Parmesan. Bake on a greased pan at 375°F for 12 minutes. Drizzle a small amount of reduced balsamic vinegar over the top before serving,

SALMON BAKED WITH PISTACHIO

Ingredients for the Salmon

2 pounds fresh salmon
4 ounces pistachios, chopped
Salt and pepper

Ingredients for the Sauce

6 ounces craisins
6 dried apples, chopped
3 cups white wine
3 ounces cold butter

Preparation for the Salmon

PREHEAT oven to 375°F.

SEASON salmon with salt and pepper, top with pistachio, and bake at 375°F until done.

Preparation for the Sauce

SIMMER craisins and apples in wine until reduced by half.

REMOVE from heat and whisk in cold butter.

Serves 4-6

FLOURLESS CHOCOLATE-ESPRESSO CAKE

Ingredients

12 ounces bittersweet chocolate	5 ounces water
4 ounces Oban Chocolate Wafers	8 ounces brown sugar
16 ounces unsalted butter	8 large whole AA eggs
4 tablespoons coffee concentrate	

Preparation

PREHEAT oven to 325°F.

BUTTER and line a 9-inch pie pan. Chop chocolates. Bring butter, brown sugar, water, and coffee concentrate to a boil. Add chocolate and stir until dissolved. Whisk in eggs. Bake at 325°F until center is set in a hot water bath with enough water to come two-thirds of the way up the side of the pan that contains batter.

CHILL cake overnight.

INVERT cake onto a cardboard circle and apply a hot towel to the bottom of the pan to loosen the cake. Pull cake pan off and re-invert the cake onto another circle.

SERVE cold with Crème Anglaise or raspberry sauce.

Serves 8-12

CRÈME ANGLAISE

Ingredients

2 cups whole milk	4 egg yolks
1 teaspoon imitation vanilla	½ cup sugar

Preparation

BRING milk and vanilla to a boil.

WHIP egg yolks and sugar until pale and thick. Temper the egg mixture with the hot milk. Return to stove and stir constantly over medium heat until:
- steam rises from sauce
- foam on top subsides
- the sauce is noticeably thicker

STRAIN the sauce through a sieve and place in a cold water bath to halt cooking.

THE *WINE SPECTATOR* AWARD

Many of the restaurants included in this cookbook have been recognized by *Wine Spectator*, the world's most popular wine magazine. It reviews more than 10,000 wines each year and covers travel, fine dining and the lifestyle of wine for novices and connoisseurs alike. Through its Restaurant Awards program, the magazine recognizes restaurants around the world that offer distinguished wine lists.

Awards are given in three tiers. In 2003, more than 3,600 restaurants earned wine list awards. To qualify, wine lists must provide vintages and appellations for all selections. The overall presentation and appearance of the list are also important. Once past these initial requirements, lists are then judged for one of our three awards: the Award of Excellence, the Best of Award of Excellence, and the Grand Award.

- **Award of Excellence**—The basic Award of Excellence recognizes restaurants with lists that offer a well-chosen selection of quality producers, along with a thematic match to the menu in both price and style.

- **Best of Award of Excellence**—The second-tier Best of Award of Excellence, was created to give special recognition to those restaurants that exceed the requirements of the basic category. These lists must display vintage depth, including vertical offerings of several top wines, as well as excellent breadth from major winegrowing regions.

- **Grand Award**—The highest award, the Grand Award, is given to those restaurants that show an uncompromising, passionate devotion to quality. These lists show serious depth of mature vintages, outstanding breadth in their vertical offerings, excellent harmony with the menu, and superior organization and presentation. In 2003, only 89 restaurants held *Wine Spectator* Grand Awards.

Chico Hot Springs

Established 1900

#1 Chico Road
Pray, Montana
1-800-HOT-WADA or 406-333-4933
www.chicohotsprings.com
chico@chicohotsprings.com

Open year-round
Nightly, 5:30 to 9:00 pm
Sunday brunch, served from
8:30 am to 11:30 am

Reservations recommended

Chico Hot Springs today.

Chico Hot Springs

Eve & Mike Art, Owners
Colin Davis, General Manager
Chris Clark, Chef

Generous verandas, period furnishings, and healing waters invite the visitor to experience turn-of-the-century hospitality under the shadow of Emigrant Peak. The Chico Hot Springs Resort and Day Spa consists of three lodges, several cabins and houses, two open-air mineral hot springs pools, two restaurants, a saloon (live bands every Friday and Saturday night year-round), a day spa, a gift shop and activity center, a full convention facility, and a horse barn. Chico has a tradition of bringing fine dining to Montana and stands out as one of the region's best restaurants.

The hot springs, long appreciated by native peoples, got their commercial start during the territorial period when miners stopped by to bathe and "wash their duds." In 1876, an inventive settler tapped into the 112-degree water, piping it under his greenhouse to grow vegetables for local residents. A hotel was planned in the 1800s, but in 1892, there were still no facilities, and families camped nearby to enjoy the springs. Percie and Bill Knowles inherited the property in 1894. They ran a boarding house for miners, and in 1900, built the long-awaited hot springs hotel. When Bill Knowles died in 1910, Percie and her son Radbourne transformed the luxurious hotel into a respected medical facility. Dr. George A. Townsend joined the staff in 1912 and under his direction, the hospital and healing waters gained renown throughout the Northwest.

After Radbourne's death in 1943, Chico Hot Springs went through a series of owners who couldn't decide whether to make it a health resort, a vacation getaway, or a combination of both. In 1973, Mike and Eve Art bought the property, and three years later they moved from Cleveland, Ohio, to live on it. Since then they've made many improvements, so that once again Bill and Percie's resort is thriving.

And reportedly, so is the ghostly activity at the old lodge. Former owner John Sterhan recalls that during his tenure from 1967 to 1972, the staff reported some strange events. The most common belief among those who have reported eerie encounters at Chico is that the Knowleses, especially Percie, have never left.

Ghosts may abound at this lovely resort, but guests at Chico are usually so busy

Chico Hot Springs in its early day; much of the old structure still remains.

20

Chico Hot Springs, Resort and Day Spa, Pray

enjoying the pleasures of scrumptious food, relaxing hot pools, and towering snowcapped peaks that they have little time left to think about the paranormal.

In 1974, Mike and Eve Art began recapturing the once-famous hotel's turn of the century ambiance. With its Georgian-inspired architecture and warm Craftsman-style interiors, Chico is one of Montana's best-preserved examples of an early 20th century hot springs hotel and health resort. In June of 1999, Chico Hot Springs was listed on the National Register of Historic Places.

The Inn specializes in fresh, exceptional cuisine, with most of the produce coming from Chico's own garden. The steaks are generous, the seafood is flown in fresh, and all of the baking is done on the premises. What's more, Chico boasts one of the region's finest wine cellars, and the wine list has gotten the *Wine Spectator* Award of Excellence five times.

It isn't surprising that Chico is a favorite "haunt" of celebrities such as Peter Fonda, Jeff Bridges, and Dennis Quaid. In the old days, Chico even hosted famed cowboy artist Charles Russell, who traded drawings on the back of stationery for drinks, and President Theodore Roosevelt, who stayed there the night before he visited Yellowstone National Park. While the dining room is popular with Montana's Hollywood contingent, it's also the locals' choice hands down.

Chico also offers year-round activities such as horseback trips, rafting, fly fishing, hiking, mountain biking, scenic floats on the Yellowstone River, cross-country skiing, dogsled treks, and much more. Only 30 minutes to Yellowstone National Park and 10 minutes to the Yellowstone River, Chico is in an ideal location—the best of everything Montana offers is just minutes away.

Chico Hot Springs, Resort and Day Spa Pray

21

OYSTERS ROCKEFELLER

Chico started serving this timeless hors d'oeuvre in 1976. It was a kind of delicacy in Montana at the time, since fresh seafood was not readily available. Still, fresh oysters were flown in once a week to Billings (about 200 miles away), and the owners would go pick up the order. Today, with fresh seafood flown in daily, it's easier to offer oysters on the menu.

Ingredients

24   East or West Coast oysters

2	cups fresh spinach, julienne		¾	cups heavy whipping cream
1	large yellow onion, diced		¼	cup Parmesan cheese, grated
2	slices bacon, julienne		¾	cup hollandaise sauce
2	tablespoons garlic, minced		2	cups coarse salt
1	tablespoon anisette liqueur			

PREHEAT oven to 450°F.

SHUCK oysters and place on the half shell.

RENDER bacon in large sauté pan. Add onions, cook until translucent. Combine garlic, spinach, anisette, and cream; mix and cook until spinach is wilted. Remove from heat.

SPOON one heaping teaspoon of spinach mixture onto each oyster, sprinkle with Parmesan. Top each oyster with a dollop of the Hollandaise Sauce, about ½ teaspoon.

PREPARE a sheet pan with a thick layer of coarse salt. Nestle the oysters in the salt. Bake for 10 minutes until the sauce is golden brown. Serve hot, straight from the oven right on the baking pan.

Hollandaise Sauce

3	eggs, yolks only		1	lemon, juiced
2	tablespoons white wine		1	teaspoon salt
½	pound and 2 tablespoons unsalted, clarified butter, 95°F		½	teaspoon cayenne pepper

MELT butter over medium heat and skim foam off top with a large spoon to prepare "clarified" butter. In a separate saucepan, add egg yolks and white wine, whisk over medium heat until the mixture thickens (about three minutes). Remove mixture from heat and slowly drizzle 95°F butter into the pan, constantly stirring. The temperature of the butter is crucial, measure it with a thermometer. Once all butter has been incorporated, add rest of ingredients, while continuing to stir. Serve with the oysters.

Serves 4

WILD MUSHROOM BISQUE

Spring brings morels and other wild mushrooms bursting from the forest floors throughout the region. If you are lucky you might catch a string of special dishes on the dining room menu prepared with an assortment of fresh fungi. This is the best of those savory recipes, though it can also be prepared with dried mushrooms.

Ingredients

- ¼ *pound fresh portabella mushrooms, grilled and chopped*
- ¼ *pound fresh oyster mushrooms, stemmed and chopped*
- ¼ *pound fresh morel mushrooms*
- 2 *large leeks, cleaned and chopped*
- ½ *large yellow onion, chopped*
- 2 *tablespoons garlic, minced*

- ½ *gallon chicken stock or broth*
- 2 *cups heavy whipping cream*
- ½ *cup sherry or white wine*
- 1 *teaspoon fresh thyme leaves*
- 2 *tablespoons unsalted butter*
  Salt and pepper to taste
- ¼ *cup Parmesan cheese, grated*
  Crostini bread

IN A LARGE stockpot sauté garlic, onions, leeks, fresh oyster, and grilled portabella mushrooms until soft. Add sherry or wine, chicken stock and cream; simmer on medium heat until reduced by one-third (about 45 minutes). Purée and return to pot. Sauté whole morels in butter, salt and pepper to taste. Serve soup with crostini (thin slices of toasted bread) and top with whole morels, Parmesan, and extra sprigs of thyme for garnish.

Chicken Stock

- 1 *small whole chicken (3 pounds)*
- 1 *whole duck (4 to 5 pounds)*
- 3 *large carrots, peeled, rough chopped*
- 6 *stalks celery, rough chopped*
- 2 *large white onions, rough chopped*
- 4 *cloves garlic, rough chopped*

- 1 *bunch parsley or stems, rough chopped*
- 3 *bay leaves*
- 1 *tablespoon black peppercorns*
- 2 *tablespoon kosher salt*

PLACE chicken and duck with organs and necks in a large stockpot (3 gallons); add other ingredients. Fill with cold water just over the top of ingredients. Simmer over medium heat for 6 to 12 hours; skim fat off top and strain. Stock keeps up to 3 days refrigerated, if not used by then it should be frozen or discarded.

Yields 1½ gallons

FRENCHED PORK CHOPS

with Cornbread Stuffing and Apple Chutney

Melding rich autumn flavors of sweet apple and spicy chiles, this pork takes on a sumptuously rustic refinement. Cut like a rack of lamb, this recipe adds a decorative flair to pork. A local butcher or even a grocery store meat department will prepare this cut for you; be sure to request a one-inch thick restaurant cut. If this is not available, use a regular pork chop.

Ingredients

4	*10-ounce frenched pork chops*	*Apple Chutney*
	Maple Cornbread Stuffing	

Maple Cornbread Ingredients

1	*cup milk*	1 ½	*cup corn meal*
1	*cup buttermilk*	3	*cups bread flour*
4	*eggs*	1	*tablespoon salt*
1 ½	*cups vegetable oil*	1	*tablespoon baking powder*
½	*tablespoon maple extract*		

Preparation for Maple Cornbread

PREHEAT oven to 350°F.

COMBINE first five ingredients in a mixing bowl and whisk to combine. Sift remaining ingredients and add to batter in bowl. Mix only enough to combine; be careful not to over-mix.

POUR into a 9 x 13-inch baking pan, sprayed with cooking spray. Bake in a 350°F oven for 30 minutes or until golden and set. Serve with honey butter.

Cornbread Stuffing Ingredients

3	*slices bacon, chopped*	¼	*cup dried cranberries*
3	*stalks celery, diced*	¼	*cup heavy whipping cream*
1	*large carrot, peeled and diced*	2	*tablespoons fresh sage, chopped*
1	*medium white onion, diced*	4	*cups Maple Cornbread*
½	*cup Madeira wine or sweet sherry*		

To make Cornbread Stuffing and Pork Chops

RENDER fat from bacon; add carrot, celery, and onion. Sauté until vegetables are soft; add Madeira, cream, cranberries, sage, and cornbread. Stir thoroughly until cornbread has soaked up all liquid and mixture sticks together.

CUT a slit into the pork chop, starting at the base of the bone and cutting lengthwise toward the center of the loin. Place one-third cup of stuffing into each chop and grill 6 to 10 minutes on each side until pork is cooked to medium well. You can also broil the meat for the same amount of time. Serve with warm Apple Chutney (recipe follows) on the side.

Apple Chutney Ingredients

2 cups apple juice concentrate	2 apples (Gala, MacIntosh, or Granny Smith), peeled and chopped
2 tablespoons Ancho chiles	
½ tablespoon cornstarch	¼ cup red onion, chopped
½ tablespoon hot water	¼ cup red pepper, seeded and chopped

To make Apple Chutney

BRING chiles and apple juice concentrate to a boil. In a separate container, combine cornstarch and hot water. Once apple juice and chiles begins to boil, add cornstarch mixture. Bring back to a boil and remove from heat.

SAUTÉ apples, onion, and pepper until soft; add apple concentrate sauce and stir. Serve warm.

Serves 4

This pleasant room would have greeted you at the turn of the century at Chico Hot Springs.

Chico's dining room today.

GRILLED AHI TUNA WITH THAI ONION SAUTÉ

With fresh fish flown in several times a week, this East-meets-West dish is possible even in Montana. Light, tangy, and spicy, it's a favorite special in the dining room.

Ingredients

1   48-ounce Ahi (yellowfin) tuna filet (also excellent with Mahi Mahi)
    Salt and pepper to taste

Thai Onion Sauté

1   large leek, clean and julienne   ¾   cup Thai vinaigrette
1   large red onion, julienne

SAUTÉ onion and leeks until soft; add vinaigrette and cook until almost dry.

SEASON tuna with salt and pepper. Grill for two to three minutes on each side to serve rare; top with Thai Onion Sauté. This dish is nice served on a bed of cooked Asian noodles, such as rice stick or Soba. Both are available in the Asian food section of grocery stores or in specialty food stores.

For Thai Vinaigrette

1   lime, juiced   ¾   cup extra virgin olive oil
1   tablespoon garlic, minced   2   teaspoons sesame oil
1   tablespoon brown sugar   1   tablespoon honey
2   cups rice wine vinegar   2   tablespoons Tabasco sauce

MIX all ingredients together and let stand overnight.

Serves 4

COCONUT ALMOND TART

This is an old favorite in the restaurant and always featured on the dessert cart. Inspired by the Almond Joy candy bar, it is a delectable combination of dark chocolate and coconut combined in a toasted almond crust.

Ingredients for the Crust

1½   cups toasted almonds
¼   cups lightly packed brown sugar

¼   cup unsalted butter, melted
     9-inch tart pan with removable bottom

Topping

¼   cup heavy whipping cream
3   tablespoons unsalted butter
2   tablespoons light corn syrup

4   ounces bittersweet chocolate, chopped
2   ounces white chocolate, chopped and melted in double boiler

Filling

½   cup canned coconut cream (such as Coco Lopez)
3   ounces white chocolate, chopped
¼   cup sour cream

¼   cup unsalted butter, cut into pieces, room temperature
1¼   cups shredded sweetened coconut, lightly packed

To make crust

PREHEAT oven to 350°F.

COARSELY chop almonds in a food processor. Add sugar and melted butter. Process the mixture until finely chopped. If you don't have a food processor, use a blender. Using plastic wrap as an aid, press mixture into the bottom and along the sides of a 9-inch tart pan with a removable bottom. Bake 10 minutes. Remove the pan from the oven and cool.

To make filling

BRING coconut cream to boil in a heavy saucepan. Reduce heat to low. Add white chocolate and stir until it is melted. Pour mixture into a medium bowl. Whisk in sour cream. Add butter and whisk until it melts into batter to a smooth consistency. Stir in shredded coconut. Chill until filling is very cold, but not set, about one hour. Spoon filling into crust, smooth top. Chill until set.

To make topping

BRING first three ingredients to a low boil in a heavy saucepan, stirring frequently. Reduce heat to low. Add bittersweet chocolate and stir until melted. Pour over tart, covering filling. Spread topping with back of spoon to cover evenly. Spoon melted white chocolate into pastry bag fitted with small tip (available in the baking section at most grocery stores). Pipe in parallel vertical lines over topping, spacing evenly. With a skewer or toothpick, drag the lines to form a decorative pattern in the chocolate. Chill and serve.

VENISON LOVERS!

Research shows that humans have been eating venison for 50,000 years. At an early point in time, man was even culling excess young male ungulates so the breeding herd would continue to flourish. (Diggers have found a preponderance of young male deer bones in caves). Westerners changed their diet beginning around 1600 when cattle, sheep, hogs, and goats became the domestic meat resource of choice because they had all that marvelous fat for keeping us warm and burning the midnight oil.

When you think of "vension," the deer species comes to mind, but did you know that vension can refer to the flesh of any big game animal used as food?

Today, many cooks are afraid to prepare venison because they have heard about its alleged dryness, toughness, and unpleasant flavor. Cooking your venison is very easy, once a few basic harvesting and cooking procedures have been learned. It contains only 3 to 5 percent fat (compared to beef at 20 percent fat) and almost no cholesterol.

Venison is a fine, delicately textured meat. Many cuts are very similar to veal. Other cuts, such as chops, look like pork. Round steaks, although smaller, have the appearance of beef. Stew meat and ground venison also resemble beef. Even though many cuts of venison look like other meats, venison has one characteristic that makes it unique. Since venison is a low or no fat-meat, during cooking it needs additional moisture.

If you purchase non-native species of venison (like axis, fallow, or red deer) or commercial elk that have been harvested and processed under state or USDA Inspections, you have no concerns about the quality of your meat. Commercial animals are thoroughly inspected for health at the time of harvest.

If you do not hunt or do not have a ready access to domestic venison, you may find farms in your area in the Yellow Pages that raise and ship venison; or go to page 206 of this book to find mail-order sources. Since it is illegal to buy, sell, or trade in deer species that are native to the United States, these ranchers have imported European, Australian, or Asian deer and bred them specifically for this market. These suppliers are USDA inspected and they will be able to provide you with the exact cuts of venison that you require. Some of these firms also market prepared venison products. Other firms have fresh venison air-shipped daily from New Zealand and Europe.

Whether we want to eat healthy chemical-free meat or we need to cut back our caloric intake, we're coming back to natural, fat-free, venison. Some say it is the meat of the 21st Century.

Boodles Restaurant

215 East Main
Historic downtown Bozeman
406-587-2901
Lunch Monday-Saturday
11:30 am to 3:00 pm

Dinner nightly at 5:30 pm
Nonsmoking

Reservations
recommended

The painting in the main dining area was completed in the 1800s and brought over from Sussex, England.

Boodles
Restaurant

W. Jackson Kent, Owner
Erik J. Nelson, Chef

Boodles is located in the heart of historic Bozeman. When you enter Boodles you are greeted by a warm, comfortable atmosphere, hardwoods, rich fabrics, period art, and a unique 1860s mahogany bar originally crafted in Philadelphia.

Boodles has received the *Wine Spectator* Award of Excellence for the past four years. They have designed a menu with culinary flair to complement natural flavors and textures. In addition to the creative preparation of the menu they are proud to offer certified handcut Angus beef, seafood, organically grown vegetables, homemade breads and pastries, and other specialties to enhance your dining experience. Whether you are looking for a snack or special dessert after a concert, handcrafted cocktails at Boodles bar, an intimate dining experience, or a private function in their wine cellar, Boodles should be on your list of destinations. As one diner who had moved to Montana from New York recently remarked, "The atmosphere, menu, wine list, and service reminds me of dining in one of New York's finest."

Boodles is located in the fourth building from the left in this early photo of Bozeman.

Intimate dining is available in Boodles wine cellar.

BUTTER LETTUCE AND ARUGULA

with Molasses Vinaigrette, topped with Roasted Turkey,
Grilled Apples, Currants, and Bacon

For the Roasted Turkey

1	4-pound boneless turkey breast		1	tablespoon pepper
2	tablespoons oil		2	teaspoon parsley flakes
1	tablespoon salt		2	teaspoon dried oregano

For the Salad

2	heads butter lettuce		8	slices bacon, cooked and chopped
2	cup arugula, washed and dried		4	apples, sliced
1	cup currants			

For the Vinaigrette

1	shallot, finely chopped		1	tablespoons molasses
3	cloves garlic, finely chopped		½	cup rice vinegar
1	teaspoon salt		2	tablespoons sesame oil
½	teaspoon black pepper		¾	cup peanut oil

Preparation for Turkey

PREHEAT oven to 400°F.

RINSE turkey and pat dry.

RUB turkey with oil and spices.

PLACE in oven at 400°F. Cook about 2 hours; until internal temperature is 160-165°F.

REMOVE from oven, let cool, and shred into long strands.

Preparation for the Vinaigrette

COMBINE first 6 ingredients in a medium bowl.

SLOWLY whisk in oils.

Preparation for the Salad

TOSS ingredients in a large bowl with the vinaigrette and turkey.

ARRANGE apples around rim of bowl or plate.

Serves 4

SESAME CRUSTED AHI TUNA

with Star Anise Basmati Rice, Braised Shitake Broth,
finished with a Wasabi Ginger Compound Butter

For Tuna

4	6-ounce pieces of Ahi tuna
3	tablespoons white sesame seeds

3   tablespoons black sesame seeds

For Rice

2	tablespoons canola oil		3	star anise
½	yellow onion, finely minced		1	cup basmati rice
1	stick cinnamon		3	cups water

For Broth

½	pound shiitake mushrooms, sliced		2	tablespoons sherry
1	tablespoons sesame oil		2	tablespoons mirin
3	tablespoons peanut oil		2	tablespoons sugar
1	shallot, thinly sliced		¼	cup soy sauce
½	cup sherry		3	cups chicken broth

For Wasabi Butter

4	ounces butter (room temperature)		1	teaspoon ginger, minced
1	tablespoon powdered wasabi		2	scallions

Preparation for Rice

IN A heavy-bottomed saucepan, with lid; sauté onion in oil over medium heat.

ADD remaining ingredients and reduce heat to low. Simmer about 20 minutes until rice is cooked and water is evaporated.

Preparation for Broth

IN A large skillet heat oil over medium-high heat and sauté mushrooms until golden brown and a nutty aroma is evident.

ADD shallot and sauté a few minutes more.

DEGLAZE pan with sherry.

ADD remaining ingredients and bring to a boil. Cook 10-15 minutes.

Preparation for Tuna

COAT one side of tuna in the mixture of black and white sesame seeds.

SEAR in a hot skillet to desired temperature.

Preparation for Wasabi Butter

CHOP scallions and ginger.

BLEND the above with wasabi into softened butter.

SHAPE mixture into desired shape and chill.

Presentation

SERVE tuna atop rice and cover with broth. Slice butter and place on tuna.

Serves 4

Bozeman's Main Street, looking southwest from an early hotel balcony.

BRAISED BISON SHORT RIBS
with Tomato and Fennel, served atop Soft Polenta

For the Ribs

2	tablespoons salt	1	bulb fennel, fronds and bulb chopped
1	tablespoon black pepper	2	stalks celery, chopped
2	teaspoons cayenne	4	cloves garlic, minced
2	teaspoon basil (dried)	1	16-ounce can chopped tomatoes
¼	cup olive oil	2	cups red wine
4	bison short rib slabs	3	cups chicken broth
1	yellow onion, julienne		

For the Polenta

½	cup yellow cornmeal	½	cup grated Parmesan
3	cup water	½	teaspoon white pepper
2	tablespoons butter	2	tablespoons salt

Preparation for Bison Short Ribs

PREHEAT oven to 450°F.

COMBINE spices and rub onto ribs. Heat oil in heavy-bottomed large casserole dish over medium-high heat. Add ribs and sear on both sides (about 3-4 minutes per side). Remove from dish.

SAUTÉ vegetables, minus the tomatoes, until soft (about 5 minutes). Deglaze pan with red wine and reduce for 5 minutes. Add tomatoes and ribs and cover with chicken broth. Cover with lid and place in oven. Check after 2 hours and add more liquid if ribs are drying. Cook 1 hour more or until tender.

Preparation for Polenta

BRING water to a boil; slowly whisk in cornmeal and reduce heat to low. Cover and stir every 5 minutes. Cook about 20 minutes. Remove from heat and stir in remaining ingredients.

To Serve

SERVE polenta on the bottom of a large pasta bowl or entrée plate with ribs on top and sauce around the polenta.

Serves 4

John Bozeman's Bistro

Established in 1983

125 West Main
Historic downtown Bozeman
406-587-4100
www.johnbozemansbistro.com

Reservations recommended
Lunch, 11:30 am to 2:30 pm
Dinner, 5:00 to 9:30 pm
Closed Mondays and Tuesdays

The chefs at John Bozeman's Bistro.

John Bozeman's Bistro

Tyler and Carla Hill, Owners
Perry Wenzel, Chef

On July 7, 1864, Daniel E. Rouse and William J. Beall drafted plans for the townsite of Bozeman, named for John Bozeman who first came to Montana in search of gold. When that didn't pan out, John decided to help the miners. In 1863, he and John Jacobs blazed the Bozeman Trail, a cutoff route from the Oregon Trail, and guided miners to Virginia City through the Gallatin Valley.

One of the restaurants inspired by this city's history is John Bozeman's Bistro, an original fine-dining experience with Montana hospitality in its one-of-a-kind setting. The imaginative "World Cuisine," fine wines, quality brews, and great service are enhanced by the unique design of the renovated 1905 downtown building. The façade of the building is a replica of the way things were in the early 1900s. Your feet will cross a floor of multicolored slate from Florence, Italy as you enter. On the west side of the restaurant are the restored 1930s booths with glass partitions to ensure your dining privacy. The original art deco lights over the granite bar hang from the 90-year-old restored ceiling. For over 20 years, the Bistro has been known as a local favorite for its creative treatment of the freshest ingredients and its international flair with a multi-dimensional flavor.

A parade marches by the location of what is now the Bistro on the west end of Bozeman's Main Street in the 1940s.

CHUNKY SUMMER GAZPACHO

Ingredients

4	cups coarsely chopped ripe tomatoes		¼	cup olive oil
2	cups chopped and peeled cucumber		¼	cup red wine vinegar
½	cup chopped green bell pepper		2	teaspoon soy sauce
½	cup chopped red bell pepper		¼	teaspoon dry oregano
1	cup finely chopped red onion		¼	teaspoon fresh ground black pepper
1	cup finely chopped celery		½	teaspoon hot sauce
¼	cup finely chopped parsley		1	teaspoon fresh minced garlic
¼	cup finely chopped fresh basil		2	teaspoon sea salt
¼	cup finely chopped mint		2	lemons, juice of
¼	cup finely chopped fresh cauliflower		1	32-ounce can of V8 juice
¼	cup capers		1	16-ounce can thick tomato sauce
¼	cup diced feta cheese			

Preparation

COMBINE all ingredients in a large bowl, stir well, cover, and chill.

GARNISH with sour cream or yogurt.

Serves 10

The inviting interior of the present-day Bistro.

MEDITERRANEAN CRAB CAKES

Ingredients

1	cup white bread crumbs	½	teaspoon dry oregano
10	ounces fresh crabmeat, Dungeness or Lump Crab	½	teaspoon dry mustard
1	teaspoon minced garlic	½	teaspoon sea salt
⅓	cup red bell peppers, minced	2	shakes Tabasco sauce
3	tablespoons, red onion minced	2	medium eggs, lightly beaten
3	tablespoons celery, minced	1	teaspoon olive oil
1	tablespoon finely chopped parsley		Lemon wedges
1	tablespoon finely chopped mushroom		

Preparation

MIX all ingredients except olive oil and lemon wedges. Heat olive oil in nonstick pan. Form crab cakes using ⅓ cup scoop, place in saucepan. Flatten and sauté on each side until lightly browned.

TRANSFER crab cakes to plate. Garnish with lemon wedge and dollop of favorite tartar sauce and serve immediately.

You can expect out-of-the-ordinary lunches at the Bistro.

Gallatin River Lodge

GALLATIN RIVER LODGE

Established 1999

9105 Thorpe Road
One mile west of State Route 85
(off Jackrabbit Lane)
Bozeman, Montana
www.grlodge.com

Open year-round for lodging
or for dinner only
406-388-0148

Bar opens at 4:30 pm
Dinner service 5:30-9:30 nightly

Gallatin River Lodge

Steve & Christy Gamble, Owners
Mitchell Kayser, Chef

The lodge at dusk.

Gallatin River Lodge, just minutes from Bozeman and Yellowstone National Park, is a year-round full-service fly-fishing lodge. The finest, most diverse fly fishing in the world is found just out the door on the Gallatin, Yellowstone, and Madison Rivers and private nearby streams.

The menu reflects influences from many different cuisines, including baked brie, Sweet Cajun Shrimp, and Bison New York Strip. Local favorites include lamb chops and steelhead trout. House-baked breads accompany each meal, and to finish things off, choose from a creative selection of desserts to tempt your sweet tooth.

"The Gallatin River Grill" is open seven nights a week to the general public as well as guests of the lodge. Chef Mitchell Kayser and Sous Chef Kris Kahao offer a new menu each week that has given the grill an exceptional reputation for dining. Entrées include certified Angus beef, buffalo, duck, pheasant, pork, lamb, and fish prepared in the style of creative Northwest American cuisine. Accorded the *Wine Spectator* Award of Excellence, the restaurant offers a nice selection of fine wines as well as a top-shelf bar to enhance your dining.

The fly tying room.

The 50-seat dining room with fir floors, oak furnishings, and a-turn of-the-century oak back bar offer a comfortable environment to enjoy a meal or a drink from the full-service bar. You can watch white-tailed deer graze by the trout pond or enjoy the spectacular views of the Spanish Peaks and Bridger Mountains while the dining room staff takes care of your every need.

Year-round service includes fine dining, conference, wedding, and catering services, and nightly bed and breakfast accommodations. Six suites are perfect for couples or anglers and contain rustic but elegant decor, fireplaces, Jacuzzi tubs, and spectacular views of the mountains and river habitat. A complete fly-fishing guide service is also available.

Pan-seared Buffalo over Spinach & Potato Gnocchi with Creamed Mushrooms

Buffalo Medallions Ingredients

2 *pounds buffalo tenderloin cut into 2-ounce medallions*
Salt and pepper to taste
1-2 *tablespoons vegetable oil*

Preparation

PREHEAT oven to 400°F. Over high heat with a little of the oil carefully place the medallions into the large ovenproof sauté pan. Cook on each side for 1 minute. Now place the pan into the oven and cook for 2-3 minutes. Pull from the oven and check for desired doneness.

Spinach and Potato Gnocchi Ingredients

2	*pounds russet potatoes*		1	*sprig minced thyme*
1½-2	*cups flour*		½	*cup spinach, wilted, dried, and minced*
3	*egg yolks*			*Salt and pepper to taste*

Preparation

BAKE the potatoes until done. Now wilt the spinach and squeeze dry. (For wilted spinach you may steam in a basket over boiling water or place spinach in a stainless bowl and place over simmering water until the spinach wilts.) Mince the spinach and thyme together. Place potatoes in a ricer and then add the spinach and thyme to the potatoes. Place the mixture on a cutting board, forming a large circle with a small well in it. Place about a cup of flour into the well. Now add the egg yolks and more flour. Mix in the potatoes with the flour and egg mixture. Keep adding flour until it is no longer sticky and it forms soft dough. Let rest for a few minutes and roll out long snake-like strands about ¼-inch thick. Cut the dough into ¾-inch pieces and roll into a ball. Using a fork, lightly press the small dough-formed balls. After you have formed the gnocchi, get a pot of salted water boiling. Place gnocchi into salted boiling water. Remember, they are done when they float. Remove from water and let cool or use right away. If you let them cool, you can reheat them with a little butter over medium heat in a sauté pan.

Creamed Mushrooms Ingredients

3   cups mushrooms, sliced

1   shallot, minced

1   clove garlic, minced

1   cup chicken stock or broth

½   cup heavy cream

Salt and pepper to taste

2-3 tablespoons vegetable oil

¼   cup white wine—or if you have it, dry vermouth works very well

Preparation

HEAT the oil in a large pot over medium heat and add the shallots. Once the shallots begin to turn clear, add the mushrooms and sauté for a couple of minutes. Now add the garlic and sauté for one more minute. Add the wine or vermouth and reduce until the liquid is almost gone. Add the chicken stock/broth and reduce by half. Finally, add the cream and salt and pepper.

Presentation

PLACE the gnocchi onto a plate, cover with the mushroom sauce, and add the medallions.

SERVE and enjoy!

Fshing in the Gallatin Canyon long ago.

The
Mint
Bar
&
Café

Established 1904

27 East Main
Belgrade, Montana
406-388-1100

Open for lunch
Monday through Friday
11:00 am to 2:00 pm

Open seven nights a week
for dinner

5:00 to 10:00 pm

Reservations recommended

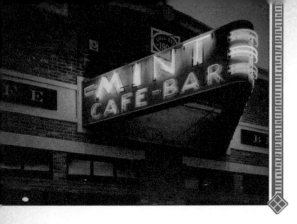

The Mint

Jay Bentley, Owner
Justin Forsberg, Chef
Charles Donch, Manager

Blanche and I first met Jay Bentley when he was the owner and chef of the Continental Divide in Ennis. We have spent many an evening with Jay at The Divide, and now at The Mint, enjoying good food and drink. As you walk into the restaurant you are greeted with the warmth of the long cowboy bar decorated with Western memorabilia. The bar has an extensive selection of single-malt scotches and a fine wine list. There are always two fresh fish entrées on the menu with a choice of two or three sauces. I recommend Jay's pork chop along with my favorite, the large New York strip. Stop in at The Mint for one of the finest dining experiences in the country and enjoy the warm Montana flavor.

The present-day Mint has survived several incarnations: a bar, a bordello, general store, and a one-lane bowling alley. At one time, patrons even played horseshoes between the historic Mint and Hub bars. In the 1970s half the building burned down and was boarded up for some time. Needless to say, the building in which The Mint resides has had quite a history.

In 1995, The Mint was restored and opened as the current establishment. After training under French chefs who prepared the kind of elaborate dishes so typical during the 1970s and '80s, owner Jay Bentley found—many years and several restaurants later—that he has become much more appreciative of simple and well prepared comfort food where ingredients and simplicity far more important than the elaborate and ostentatious creations of his youth.

When he opened THE MINT BAR & CAFÉ in 1995, having opened many restaurants over the years, Jay was determined to keep it simple, consistent, and good. He wanted The Mint to be known as more of a neighborhood place with great food, like the places he used to love, and still does, in New Orleans. He doesn't spend much time in the kitchen any more, but he watches most of the food that his chefs put out. Since the age of fifteen, Chef Justin Forsberg has been working with Jay. Justin is a creative and energetic young man who is doing a wonderful job of balancing Jay's concept of culinary comfort with his own desire to experiment with new and interesting ideas. Jay's hard-working and friendly staff will always make sure that your dining experience is memorable.

Garlic and Caraway Seed Roasted Pork Loin Medallions
with Bread Dumplings and Onion Gravy

For the Pork Loin

2	pounds pork loin roast		2	tablespoons garlic, chopped
2	tablespoons kosher salt		2½	cups beef stock
2	tablespoons caraway seeds			

PREHEAT oven to 350°F.

TRIM excess fat from the pork if desired. In a small bowl, mix salt, garlic, and caraway seeds, and liberally crust the top side of the loin. Transfer the pork to a medium-sized roasting pan and add the beef stock to the bottom. Roast in a preheated oven for 90 minutes or until desired doneness is achieved and the top is golden brown. Remove from pan and save the liquid for the gravy.

For the Bread Dumplings

16	cups of day-old bread cut into 1-inch cubes		1	cup yellow onion, diced
5	eggs		1	cup celery hearts (white portion), diced
½	cup milk		1	teaspoon salt
3	tablespoons whole salted butter		½	teaspoon white pepper
2	teaspoons chicken base dissolved in two tablespoons of warm water		1	pinch nutmeg

COMBINE all ingredients into food processor or large bowl and mix slowly until bread is soft and all ingredients are thoroughly mixed together. Roll into balls slightly smaller than tennis balls and refrigerate for 1 hour. Bring a medium sauce pot with 4 inches of water to a boil, and then reduce to a simmer. Add dumplings to water and cook slowly for 20-25 minutes. Remove from water and let drain.

For the Onion Gravy

2	large yellow onions, julienne		Leftover liquid from pork loin
3	tablespoons bacon or duck fat		Salt and pepper to taste
4	tablespoons flour		

COMBINE onions and fat in a medium saucepan over high heat and sauté until onions become golden brown. Stir in flour until it has all been absorbed, then slowly add liquid saved from the pork loin (if not enough, use a little beef stock) and mix constantly until gravy comes to boil. Season with salt and pepper.

SERVE two, 4-ounce slices of pork with two dumplings and gravy over the top.

Serves 4

Southwest Spice-Blackened Bison Ribeye
with a Sweet Chipotle Vinaigrette

For the Ribeye

4	12-ounce or larger, boneless bison ribeye steaks	Worcestershire sauce
	Lemon pepper	Canola oil

AT LEAST 6 hours in advance, marinate the ribeyes with a light coating of lemon pepper, a few splashes of Worcestershire, and just enough canola oil to coat the steaks. Keep refrigerated.

Sweet Chipotle Vinaigrette

2	tablespoons Dijon mustard	½	cup apple cider vinegar
2	teaspoons cumin	1	tablespoon Worcestershire sauce
2	tablespoons brown sugar	1	teaspoon pepper
4	whole chipotle chiles in mole sauce	1½	cups canola oil

COMBINE all ingredients except canola oil in a blender or food processor and mix until all ingredients have been incorporated. While still blending, slowly pour in canola oil so that it combines with the other ingredients and doesn't separate. Refrigerate an hour.

Southwest Spice

2	tablespoons paprika	1	teaspoon cinnamon
1	tablespoon oregano	1	teaspoon coriander
1	tablespoon onion powder	1	teaspoon chile powder
1	tablespoon garlic powder	½	teaspoon cayenne pepper
1	tablespoon cumin		

PREHEAT oven to 400°F.

MIX all spices together. Remove ribeyes from marinade and liberally apply spice mixture to the top side of the steak. Then, in a cast-iron skillet that is extremely hot, place the steaks with the spice side down for about a minute or until the spices have been burnt onto the steak and are smoking. Then transfer the steaks to the preheated oven for 15 minutes to achieve medium rare doneness (or leave in longer if so desired). Serve with the vinaigrette on the side in a small ramekin to dip the meat into.

Serves 4

CAST-IRON ROASTED PHEASANT
with Pancetta and Juniper Sauce

For the Pheasant

2	whole pheasants	2	tablespoons lemon pepper
2	tablespoons cracked black pepper		Olive oil
3	tablespoons butter		

PREHEAT oven to 400°F.

REMOVE both wings from each pheasant and split down the middle through the breast and then through the backbone. Sprinkle an even layer of peppercorns and lemon pepper over the skin of the pheasant and place in a bowl large enough to hold all the halves and then lightly coat with the oil. Let this marinate for 1 hour. Place a large cast-iron skillet big enough to hold all the pheasants in the oven for 30 minutes so that it is smoking hot. Melt the butter in the skillet and immediately place the pheasants skin side down in the butter and place skillet back in oven. Cook for 20 minutes or until skin is golden brown and the flesh is cooked enough that no blood drains out when poked with a knife.

For the Pancetta and Juniper Sauce

½	pound diced pancetta (or slab bacon if pancetta unavailable)	2	tablespoons gin
3	tablespoons flour	1	tablespoon ground dried juniper berries
2	minced shallots	2	tablespoons whole butter
2	cups chicken stock or broth		Salt and pepper to taste
½	cup dry white wine		Chopped parsley

COOK the pancetta in a hot sauce pan until browned and crispy. Remove from pan leaving the drippings behind and use this to sauté the shallots until they are translucent. Add the flour and mix together so that a roux is formed. Whisk in chicken stock slowly so that no lumps form. Add wine, gin, and juniper berries and bring to a boil to thicken the sauce. After desired consistency is achieved, remove from heat and stir in the whole butter to make the sauce creamy and give it a nice sheen. Adjust the flavor with salt and pepper and add chopped parsley for color. Serve pheasants with skin side up and spoon the sauce around the base them to keep the skin crispy.

Serves 4

BARBECUE SHRIMP

When I was apprenticing at the Louis XVI in New Orleans in the eighties, the menu was classic French. For those of us in the kitchen who had to cook that kind of food every night, we quickly grew tired of the creams and ornate presentation involved in their preparation. Our favorite foods became the everyday kind of neighborhood food favored by average New Orleanians. Barbecued shrimp always ranked near the top along with gumbo, red beans, and rice.

This is the greatest shrimp recipe I have ever eaten. Actually the shrimp isn't really grilled, but cooked in a spicy olive oil and butter sauce. The original recipe came from Pascale's Manale Restaurant in New Orleans and there are all kinds of variations, but I like this one the best. —Jay Bentley

For the Shrimp

2 pounds large fresh or frozen shrimp in the shell (heads on if possible)

2 sticks butter (1 cup)

1 cup olive or vegetable oil

4-6 bay leaves, crumbled

2 tablespoons minced garlic

3 teaspoons crushed rosemary

1 teaspoon basil

1 teaspoon oregano

½ teaspoon kosher or sea salt

1 tablespoon black pepper

1 tablespoon paprika

1 teaspoon lemon juice

2 tablespoons Worcestershire sauce

Preparation

PREHEAT oven to 400°F.

IN A sauté pan, melt the butter and oil then all of the ingredients except the shrimp. Cook until the sauce begins to boil then remove from the heat and let it stand to room temperature. Add the shrimp and allow them to marinate for an hour in the sauce before cooking. Put the pan containing the shrimp into the preheated oven for around 18 minutes or until they turn pink. Do not overcook! You can also cook this on top of the stove over high heat. Remove when they turn pink and serve with lots of good bread.

Serves 4

Buck's T-4 Lodge

U.S. Highway 191, (one mile south of the Big Sky spur road)
Big Sky, Montana
1-800-822-4484 or 406-995-4111
Open seasonally winter and summer

Dining 7 days/week 6:00 to 9:30 pm
info@buckst4.com
www.buckst4.com
Lodging available

Buck's T-4 Lodge
A Big Sky Tradition

Mike Scholz, Owner
David O'Conner, General Manager
Scott Peterson, Chef

Buck's T-4 wine room.

Buck's T-4 began as a hunting lodge in 1946, eventually growing into one of southwest Montana's favorite roadhouses. Buck and Helen Knight opened the business with a philosophy of home-cooked food and genuine, friendly service. Buck's "Lazy T-4" brand became synonymous with friends, food, and fun in Gallatin Canyon. Mike Scholz purchased the lodge from the Knights in 1972, and has kept that philosophy interwoven in his business today.

The original bar that Buck Knight built in 1952 from local lodgepole pine is the oldest part of the complex and is still in use today, with many of Helen's special touches. There is even a large game room with video games and pool tables.

The adjoining bar was constructed in 1972 using two adjacent cabins, turning each 90 degrees and framing them in together. The construction was accomplished by Buck and a few friends using wood from the property. The tongue-and-groove ceiling, handmade bar, and unpeeled log accents exemplify the style and craftsmanship of mid-century rural Montana. Great care has been taken to preserve the original construction and feel of the building.

A new dining room adjacent to the original bar was also built in 1972, as well as a large dance hall, which soon became known as one of Montana's raucous and rowdy roadhouses. Large dances were held most weekends in the mid to late seventies, often featuring Montana's Mission Mountain Wood Band. In subsequent years, a lounge, three private dining rooms and a large dining room addition, display wine cellar, and state-of-the-art kitchen

Buck's T-4 in 1972.

were added. Later, a more casual restaurant opened, featuring pizza and hamburgers with pool tables and video games. While the dance hall now holds more weddings than wildness, and the restaurant sees more culinarians than cowboys, Buck's T-4 still has echoes of its roadhouse past.

Mike believes in providing the best possible cuisine and service for guests, while retaining the original Montana ambiance that started with the Knights. He feels that culinary excellence and pretension do not necessarily go hand-in-hand.

The combination of Mike's unwavering dedication to providing superior dining for his guests and the chef's culinary artistry has created a top-notch experience. Their approach is the application of classical techniques to traditional local ingredients. Some of the game meats he has featured include South Dakota bison, South Texas antelope, New Zealand red deer, North American wapiti (elk) and Alaskan caribou. In 1999, Buck's T-4 was invited to participate at the prestigious James Beard Foundation in New York. Buck's has the honor of being the first restaurant from Montana to be invited. While the Buck's T-4 menu focuses on wild game, his guests also enjoy the hand-cut steaks, seafood, and other unique creations.

Located in the shadow of Lone Peak and the Big Sky Ski and Summer Resort, and but a stone's throw from Yellowstone National Park, the Big Sky community is swiftly becoming one of the most popular vacation destinations in Montana. Visitors enjoy all the excitement the Rocky Mountains have to offer, including whitewater rafting, hiking, horseback riding, and fly fishing in the renowned blue-ribbon waters of the Gallatin River. Big Sky also offers world-class skiing in the winter, having grown to be the fourth largest ski area in the United States.

Buck's T-4 today.

Chef Scott Peterson.

WILD GAME MEATLOAF

Ingredients

1 cup red onion, fine diced	1 teaspoon white ground pepper
1 cup green onion, fine diced	½ teaspoon cayenne pepper
½ cup carrot, fine diced	1½ teaspoon ground cumin
⅓ cup celery stalk, fine diced	1 teaspoon ground nutmeg
⅓ cup green bell pepper, fine diced	3 pounds wild game trim, ground
⅓ cup red bell pepper, fine diced	1 pound bulk pork sausage
1 tablespoon peeled clove garlic, finely chopped	⅓ cup ketchup
1 tablespoon kosher salt	1 cup crouton crumbs
1½ teaspoon freshly-ground black peppercorn	2 tablespoons butter
	4 large eggs
	⅓ cup half-and-half

Method

PREHEAT oven to 375°F.

SAUTÉ vegetables and garlic in butter until al dente. Cool to below 40°F.

PLACE ground game trim in mixer with pork sausage, cooled vegetables, spices, ketchup, and crouton crumbs. Place dough hook on mixer and mix on low speed. Add eggs, one at a time. If no mixer is available, knead by hand until fully incorporated. Add half-and-half to meat mixture.

PLACE mixture into two bread pans, making sure bottom is free of any air pockets and top is smooth and domed in the center, then individually wrap each meatloaf with foil.

BAKE at 375°F in a water bath until internal temperature of meatloaf reaches 155°F.

REMOVE meatloaf from water bath, unwrap and pour off excess grease. Remove from bread pans, slice, and serve with Marinated Tomato & Roasted Garlic Sauce (recipe follows).

Makes two loaves

MARINATED TOMATO & ROASTED GARLIC SAUCE

Ingredients

1¼	pound Roma tomatoes, medium dice
3	ounces whole-peeled garlic cloves (about 18 cloves)
¼	cup olive oil
¼	ounce fresh basil chiffonade (shredded)

2	shallots, finely diced
3	ounces tomato paste
1	ounce balsamic vinegar
	Salt and pepper to taste

Method

COMBINE garlic cloves and olive oil in saucepan and simmer on low until garlic is soft, but do not allow garlic to brown, as it will become bitter. Set aside.

COMBINE tomatoes, shallots, basil, tomato paste, and balsamic vinegar. Pour warm browned garlic and olive oil over tomato mixture. Stir to combine. Season with salt and pepper. Refrigerate.

BRING to room temperature before serving or warm in a microwave.

SMOKED CORN RELISH

Ingredients

12	ears of smoked corn
1	green pepper, diced
1	medium onion, diced
4	Roma tomatoes, diced
1	cup granulated sugar (reduce sugar to ½ cup if grilling)

1-1¼	cups cider vinegar
1	teaspoon turmeric
1	teaspoon yellow mustard seed
	Salt and pepper to taste

Method

SMOKE or grill corn on gas or charcoal barbecue grill, brushing with maple syrup and grilling on all sides until kernels are tender.

CUT corn kernels from cobs and combine all ingredients and simmer half an hour. Adjust to desired consistency with cornstarch.

NEW ZEALAND RED DEER

Ingredients

4	5-ounce red deer loins	16	ounces port wine
3	shallots, minced	½	cup chopped fresh thyme
¼	cup sugar	4	tablespoons whole butter, cubed
1	clove garlic, chopped		

For the Port Wine Sauce

ADD shallots to sauté pan, then sugar. Allow mixture to caramelize over low heat and add garlic and port wine, and then ¼ cup of the thyme. Reduce mixture until a syrupy consistency is obtained, or until approximately 4 ounces remain. Whisk in cold butter, one piece at a time until emulsified. Press through a fine strainer and reserve.

For the Red Deer

SEASON red deer with salt and pepper and remaining chopped thyme. Sear both sides in a hot sauté pan to medium rare (about 3 minutes per side). Be careful not to exceed medium, as the meat will become chewy and take on a strong game flavor. Slice and fan on a bed of the Port Wine Sauce. Serve with a napoleon made of alternating layers of Wild Rice Griddle Cakes (see accompanying recipe) and sautéed spinach.

Serves 4

WILD RICE GRIDDLE CAKES

Ingredients

1	cup cooked wild rice	2	green onions, minced
½	cup carrot, small dice	1	cup buttermilk
¼	cup yellow onion, small dice	¼	cup pure maple syrup
¼	cup celery, small dice	¼	cup wild rice flour
1	tablespoon Roquefort cheese	½	cup all-purpose flour
1	large whole egg	¼	teaspoon baking powder

Preparation

SAUTÉ carrot, celery, and onion until soft. Add Roquefort and melt. Allow to cool, then combine with egg, green onions, maple syrup, wild rice, and buttermilk. Stir in both flours and baking powder until incorporated. Add salt and pepper to taste. Spoon onto hot griddle and cook each side as with pancakes.

Serves 4

WILD GAME PATÉ

Ingredients

½ pound peeled shallots, chopped

¾ tablespoons butter, melted

½ tablespoon fresh sage

1 tablespoon fresh thyme

5 pounds wild game trim (can use any red game meat)

1¼ pound wild boar bacon

¾ pound pork fat

1 tablespoon kosher salt

1 tablespoon ground black pepper

½ quart heavy whipping cream

4 large eggs

¾ cup brandy

1¼ cup whole roasted pistachios

Thin-sliced pancetta or prosciutto

Method

PREHEAT oven to 350°F.

ROAST pistachios in oven until slightly browned, then cool. Saute shallots in butter with sage and thyme over medium heat and cool.

DOUBLE grind wild game trim, boar bacon, and pork fat, first with ⅜-inch plate, then with ¼-inch plate. Slightly frozen meat works best. Add meat, shallots, and remaining ingredients to mixer and mix with paddle. If no mixer is available, knead mixture with hands until fully incorporated. Allow mixture to rest in refrigerator overnight so flavors can mellow and incorporate.

The Following Day

LINE loaf pans with pancetta or prosciutto. Fill pans with raw paté mixture and top with more pancetta. Wrap each loaf pan in aluminum foil. Fill a large roasting pan half full of water. Place loaf pans in this water bath and bake at 350°F for about 1½ hours, or until internal temperature reaches 145°F and juices are running clear. Remove paté from oven.

APPLY weight to each paté by placing an empty loaf pan in each, then a sheet pan over both and about 60 pounds of weight on the sheet pan. Let cool overnight.

TO SERVE, slice into wedges and serve with sourdough bread, lingonberry sauce, huckleberry mustard, and stone-ground mustard.

Makes 2 loaves

RUSSIAN CREAM WITH RASPBERRIES

Ingredients

½	tablespoon gelatin (Knox, e.g.)	⅔	tablespoon vanilla
2	ounces water	1	pounds sour cream
2	cups regular whipping cream	2	ounces raspberries per person
1	cup sugar		

Method

PLACE gelatin in water and dissolve over low flame until clear. In a large saucepan, heat cream and sugar over low flame until sugar melts and mixture is hot. Add vanilla, then gelatin. Stir mixture vigorously with wire whisk until gelatin is thoroughly dissolved and well-mixed. Remove from heat and add sour cream, mixing continuously with whisk. Place in large container and cool until firm (preferably overnight).

SERVE in a parfait glass (a wine glass works as well), layered with raspberries (most kinds of berries work very well). Top with fresh whipped cream and a French rolled wafer. Alternate garnishes might include shaved white or dark chocolate, cinnamon or nutmeg, fresh mint, frozen mango, or peach slices.

Serves 10

WHITE CHOCOLATE CHEESECAKE

Ingredients

2	pounds cream cheese	7	large eggs, separated
6	ounces unsalted butter	2	cups sugar
2	ounces pure vanilla	½	cup water
17	ounces white chocolate		Vanilla wafer crust

Method

MELT white chocolate over double-boiler. Separate eggs and melt butter. Soften cream cheese in electric mixer, add melted butter, egg yolks, vanilla, and melted white chocolate. Beat until light and fluffy, then set aside. Boil water with sugar until light brown. Beat egg whites to soft peaks, then add water-sugar mixture. Whip until stiff. Fold the two mixtures together, pour into a vanilla wafer crust and freeze until set.

Serves 16 (one cake)

Lone Mountain Ranch

Lone Mountain Ranch

Discovery is in our nature.

Established 1915

Lone Mtn. Ranch Access Rd.,
Spur 64 west off Hwy. 191
Big Sky, Montana
406-995-2782
Reservations, 1-800-514-4644
Breakfast, 8:00 am to 9:30 am

Lunch, 11:30 am to 1:30 pm
Dinner, 6:30 pm
Open seasonally December to April
and June to October 15
www.lmranch.com

Dining lodge.

Lone Mountain Ranch

Bob & Vivian Schaap, Owners
Steve Pedalino, Chef

Bob and Vivan Schaap,
Brian and Kelli Wadsworth

Lone Mountain Ranch is rich in the history of Montana. First homesteaded in 1915 as a working cattle and hay ranch, it was purchased in 1926 by Fred Butler, a Chicago paper mill tycoon who built some of the guest cabins still in use. The B-K, as the ranch was called then, was a showplace for the owner's extensive Native American artifact collection. Through the years, the ranch was a logging camp, a boy's ranch, and finally a guest ranch. Bob and Vivian Schaap have owned it since the spring of 1977, hosting guests from all over the world.

The current dining lodge, with its massive stone fireplace, was completed in 1989. The huge chandeliers are made from antlers naturally dropped each winter by bull elk. The Native American artifacts that adorn the walls are from the original B-K collection. In the charming saloon, there is a copper bar and fireplace, a naturally formed curved log that caps the bar, and a huge bull moose watching over everyone.

The Lone Mountain Ranch Dining Room is a wonderfully informal and comfortable non-smoking room. The food has received accolades from guests and has been enthusiastically reviewed in many national publications such as *Town and Country*, *Travel and Leisure*, *The New York Times*, and *The Los Angeles Times*.

One winter night weekly the ranch guests are transported via horse-drawn sleigh to the remote North Fork cabin for a very special dinner cooked on an old fashioned wood-fired cook stove.

A prime rib dinner is served family-style in a room illuminated by kerosene lanterns. Guitar music and songs round out an evening reminiscent of times long ago.

Lone Mountain dining is best described as creative American regional cuisine. Menus may include venison, lamb, bison, salmon, and duck as well as prime rib, ribeye steaks, pasta specials, and fresh fish flown in daily.

Draft horses take guests to the North Fork cabin.

Interior of dining lodge where guests gather for meals.

Lone Mountain Ranch, Big Sky

BEEF TENDERLOIN
with Mushroom Stuffing and Port Wine Sauce

Montana beef is legendary and this presentation has been a favorite with guests for several years. The wine sauce adds just the right finish. Serve with squash or other fresh vegetable and a green salad and you will have a special meal.

Ingredients

1 slice smoked bacon, finely chopped	4 8-ounce filet mignons
2 portabella mushroom caps, chopped	2 tablespoons oil
½ cup white button mushrooms, sliced	Kosher salt
2 teaspoons butter	Ground black pepper
1 teaspoon chopped garlic, finely chopped	Flour for dusting
2 teaspoons fresh rosemary, chopped	

For the Port Wine Sauce (yields one cup)

1 cup ruby port wine	1 cup demi-glace
1 tablespoon finely chopped shallot	Kosher salt and ground black pepper

Preparation for Beef Tenderloin & Mushroom Stuffing

PREHEAT oven to 400°F. Add the bacon to a cold 10-inch skillet and heat over medium-high heat. Cook until brown. Stir in mushrooms, butter, garlic, and rosemary and cook until mushrooms are tender, about 5 minutes. Drain off any liquid and place mushroom mixture into the food processor. Pulse a few times, finely chopping (but not puréeing) the mixture. Remove and season with salt and pepper.

CUT a 1-inch incision in the center (from the side, not the top) of the filet from top to bottom. Work the knife from side to side, trying to split the steak in half without actually doing so. You don't want to come through the sides and you don't want your incisions too wide or the stuffing won't stay in.

STUFF the pocket from both ends with the mushroom mixture until full, but not bulging, about 2 tablespoons per filet. Season the filet with salt and pepper and lightly dust with flour.

HEAT a large ovenproof skillet over high heat. Add 2 tablespoons of oil and when hot, add the filets, searing both sides until brown, about 3 minutes per side. Place pan in the preheated oven to finish, about 8-10 minutes for medium rare. Let rest 5 minutes before serving.

For the Port Wine Sauce

BOIL the port wine with the shallot until liquid is reduced to ¼ cup. Stir in demi-glace; cook to desired consistency. Taste, then season with salt and pepper if necessary.

Serves 4

PAN-FRIED PHEASANT BREASTS
with Pancetta, Leek, and Whole Grain Mustard Gravy

Many guests enjoy wild game dishes featuring pheasant, elk, and bison while at Lone Mountain Ranch. This flavorful presentation of pheasant has been a special request in our dining room for a number of years.

Ingredients

6	large frenched pheasant breasts	1	teaspoon thyme
2	ounces olive oil	1	teaspoon cumin
1	cup flour	1	teaspoon white pepper
2	teaspoons salt		

For the Country Gravy (Whole Grain Mustard Gravy)

1	cup pancetta, diced	1	quart milk
1	tablespoon garlic leek, white part only, diced	½	pound butter
		½	cup flour
2	tablespoons whole grain mustard		Salt and cracked black pepper to taste
1	tablespoon Dijon mustard		

For the Pheasant

PREHEAT oven to 400°F.

COMBINE all dry ingredients. Dredge pheasant breasts in flour mixture. Add oil to hot skillet, add pheasant breasts and brown. Finish in a 400°F oven for about 12-15 minutes.

For the Gravy

ADD pancetta to a cold saucepan. Render over medium heat until pancetta has browned. Add garlic leek and sauté. Add milk and whisk in mustard. In a separate pan, melt butter and whisk in flour to obtain a smooth velvety roux. Bring milk mixture to a boil and whisk in roux slowly. Continue to simmer and whisk gravy for five minutes. Season with salt and cracked black pepper to taste. (This sauce is also great with chicken or pork.) Serve pheasant breasts with a wild rice pilaf and finish with the Whole Grain Mustard Gravy.

Serves 6

GINGER MANGO SALSA

This is a hit with summer guests as a refreshing accompaniment to chicken, pork, or fish. Asian-influenced dishes are always popular.

Ingredients

2	large ripe mangos, diced	1	bunch cilantro, chopped
1	tablespoon fresh ginger, diced very fine	1	red onion, diced
1	teaspoon garlic, chopped	1	ounce rice wine vinegar
2	tablespoons roasted red pepper	1	tablespoon lemon juice

Preparation Instructions

COMBINE all ingredients and let stand for an hour before serving.

SMOKED CHEDDAR AND POBLANO CORNBREAD
Lone Mountain Ranch - Signature Dish

During the summer, we have a weekly barbecue early in the week so guests can meet our crew and each other. This cornbread has been a favorite over the years, served with grilled steak, chicken, spicy baked beans, and other barbecue delights.

Ingredients

3½	cups cornmeal	2	teaspoons baking soda
2	tablespoons sugar	1	cup smoked Cheddar, shredded
2	teaspoons salt	2	poblanos or jalapeños, diced
2	teaspoons baking powder		

Preparation

PREHEAT a cast-iron skillet in 375°F oven. Mix cornbread ingredients in a bowl. Remove hot cast-iron skillet from oven. Quickly add one tablespoon butter to the skillet, pour in the cornbread batter and return to oven. Bake for about 20 minutes (until firm).

Serves 16

TOMATO GORGONZOLA SOUP

Nordic skiing builds hearty appetites, and two kinds of soup are served on our lunch buffet each day along with freshly baked bread. This is a special favorite with guests in the winter.

Ingredients

2	tablespoons garlic, finely chopped	4	cups diced tomatoes with juice
1½	cup carrots, diced	2	cups heavy cream
1½	cup white wine	1½	cups Gorgonzola cheese
½	gallon vegetable stock or broth		Salt and pepper to taste
	Fresh basil for garnish		Olive oil

Preparation

SAUTÉ the garlic and diced carrots in some olive oil. Add the white wine and reduce by three-fourths. Add vegetable stock and tomatoes and simmer an hour. Purée the mix in a blender. Add heavy cream and Gorgonzola to the blended mix and simmer for half an hour. Salt and pepper to taste and finish with fresh basil.

Yields 2 quarts

Cross-country skiing is a 25-year tradition at Lone Mountain Ranch.

The Timbers
at Moonlight Lodge

Exit Highway 191 south into Big Sky entrance; drive 10 miles west to Moonlight Lodge entrance

Open seasonally,
Thanksgiving to April
Mid-June to end of September

Lunch, 11:30 am to 2:30 pm
Dinner, 5:30 to 9:30 pm
(Closed Mondays and Tuesdays in summer)
406-995-7777
www.moolightbasin.com

The Timbers
at Moonlight Lodge

Quinn & Emily Johnsen and
Monte & Nancy Johnsen, Owners
Scott Mechura, Executive Chef

Acquired by the Northern Pacific Railroad in 1864, the land was logged in the 1980s before being sold to the partners of Moonlight Basin Ranch. Perhaps ironically, this recent logging actually laid the groundwork for the ecological renewal now underway. Clearing these dense, biologically uniform stands of lodgepole pine created meadows and grasslands. Working in concert with conservation agencies, Moonlight Basin Ranch is developing a master plan to conserve this natural character—from protecting elk calving habitat to maintaining overall biodiversity. Originally consisting of 25,000 acres, Moonlight Basin Ranch's vision has focused on placing nearly 85 percent of the Jack Creek Drainage into conservation easements, green space, and wildlife corridors.

Today, Moonlight Basin Ranch is a luxury mountain community that offers the finest of recreation opportunities while preserving the best of Montana's grandeur, providing first-class accommodations, including townhomes, homesites, cabins, and conservation parcels while restoring and protecting wildlife corridors, open spaces and the beauty of Big Sky Country.

Located at the base of the Powder River Ski Run at Big Sky Resort, the lodge blends Western charm with unparalleled amenities, including a fine restaurant, first-class spa, wonderful lounge, bar, gourmet deli, and retail offerings that rival the best resort towns.

The lodge's "Great Room" showcases a spectacular fireplace, elegant furnishings, and breathtaking views of Lone Mountain. The Timbers Restaurant features fine cuisine, while the Timbers Bar and the Lounge offer the perfect place to relax after a long day on the slopes or pause to enjoy the surroundings. Visitors can lounge in the indoor-access pool or hot tub while gazing at the beautiful Montana landscape and Lone Peak.

The lodge also features a summer trout pond/winter ice skating rink; a sweeping outdoor deck for dining, visiting, or relaxing; gourmet deli for sandwiches, soups, and fine foods; and a retail space for the most discriminating shopper. In addition, four penthouse suites are perched atop the 36,000-square-foot lodge.

The Timbers Restaurant offers a comfortably sophisticated dining experience at Moonlight Lodge. Chef Scott Mechura brings to Big Sky over 16 years of experience in Minneapolis's finest restaurants. Scott specializes in a wide range of creative American classics with a metropolitan accent, including beef tenderloin, lamb and duck, yellowtail tuna, and venison (menu items change seasonally). Restaurateurs Quinn and Emily Johnsen and Monte and Nancy Johnsen bring their close family ties to Moonlight to ensure that The Timbers will provide an exceptional dining experience with spectacular cuisine.

For breakfast, lunch, and dinner, visit the Timbers Deli, open from 10:00 am until 3:00 pm (closed Mondays). The gourmet deli provides delectable sandwiches, soups, fine wines, and cheeses. Come in and enjoy a scrumptious meal for seating outside, or watch ice skaters on the skating rink.

The Timbers at Moonlight Lodge, nestled in the northern slope of majestic Lone Peak Mountain, is an unparalleled location for Montana weddings, receptions, or other special occasions. For outdoor celebrations, you'll enjoy the beautiful deck, the fishing pond, and breathtaking views. Executive chef Scott Mechura specializes in hearty mountain cuisine with a sophisticated flare.

The Timbers dining room.

There are fabulous views for outside dining.

GRILLED 13 MILE FARM* LEG OF LAMB
With Truffle Parsnip Purée, Asparagus, and Mint Aioli

Many people still enjoy mint with their lamb, and this is the Timbers's creative way of serving mint and lamb together.

For the Lamb

At our restaurant we use 13 Mile Farm lamb from Belgrade. We break down the legs into each of the seven muscles and then grill them.

For the Purée

10	parsnips, peeled and cut into 1-inch chunks
2	tablespoons soft butter

⅓	cup heavy cream
1	tablespoon truffle oil
	Salt and pepper to taste

STEAM parsnips until completely tender. Mash like you would potatoes. Add the softened butter, the heavy cream, the truffle oil, and salt and pepper to taste.

For the Mint Aioli

2	egg yolks
1	tablespoon lemon juice

½	cup finely diced mint
1	cup grapeseed oil

PLACE yolks and lemon juice in a bowl and, while whisking constantly, slowly add oil until mixture is white and creamy like mayonnaise. Add salt and pepper to taste and the mint. Serve on top of sliced lamb.

Serves 4

*The 13-Mile Farm in Belgrade, Montana sells certified organic whole, half, and selected cuts of lamb and grass-fed beef as well as wool products such as blankets, sweaters, hats, fleece, and yarn. (406-388-4945; www.lambandwool.com)

WARM QUAIL SALAD
With Mangos, Figs, and Honey Rosemary Vinaigrette

Ingredients

4	4-ounce quails
2	ripe mangos

½	pound mixed greens
12-15	black mission figs, dried

Preparation

PEEL mangos and slice in half, avoiding large oval pit inside. Slice each half into slivers and set aside. Slice the figs in half and set those aside as well.

RUB quails with olive oil, salt, and pepper. Grill until just cooked through inside the breast area. Slice quail in half and place on top of greens with the sliced mangos, figs, and vinaigrette.

For the Vinaigrette

4	cups grapeseed oil
2	tablespoons champagne vinegar (or any white vinegar)
3	tablespoons honey

1	teaspoon soy sauce
1	tablespoon fresh rosemary, finely chopped
	Salt and white pepper to taste

COMBINE all ingredients in blender and purée until smooth and combined.

Serves 4

BEET SALAD
Thinly sliced Red Beets with Roasted Golden Beets, Watercress, and Olive Oil

Ingredients

4	medium-sized red beets, washed and peeled
4	medium-sized golden beets, washed
¾	cup olive oil

½	pound watercress, washed and stems removed
1	12-ounce bottle white truffle oil (if available in your area)

PREHEAT oven to 350°F. Slice the red beets as thin as possible and marinate with just enough of the olive oil to coat. Set aside. Rub the golden beets with a bit more of the olive oil, some salt and pepper, and roast approximately 1½ hours until they slide off of a paring knife like a potato. Let cool and slice into wedges. Lay out red beets on plate. Toss roasted golden beets, watercress, salt and pepper, a bit of the olive oil, and truffle oil to moisten and place on top of the red beets.

Serves 6

CHOCOLATE PEANUT BUTTER GANACHE
with White Chocolate Creme Anglaise and House-Made Grape Jelly

For the Ganache

½ pound bittersweet chocolate	5 egg yolks
½ pound butter, diced	4 whole eggs
3 ounces cake flour	4 ounces peanut butter
5 ounces granulated sugar	

PREHEAT oven to 375°F.

MELT chocolate and butter over low heat, stirring constantly. Add sugar and flour and fold in. Next, add egg yolks and eggs. Mix in. Butter six 6-ounce ramekins and fill with batter. Chill overnight. The next day, scoop a hole out of the center using a melon baller or a teaspoon. Place scoop of peanut butter inside and replace scoop of chocolate. Bake for 6 minutes at 375°F. Rotate in oven and bake for 6 more minutes. Serve immediately with a spoonful of quality fruit preserve* and White Chocolate Crème Anglaise. When cut into, the chocolate and peanut butter should ooze out.

For the White Chocolate Crème Anglaise

1 vanilla bean	1 cup sugar
3 cups heavy cream	5 ounces white chocolate
8 egg yolks	

STEEP cream with the bean and ½ cup of sugar.

WHISK yolks with the other ½ cup of sugar and temper into warm cream.

CHOP the chocolate finely and pour mixture over chocolate, whisking until chocolate is melted.

STRAIN the sauce and cool.

Serves 6

This is the signature dish of our restaurant. However, for ease in making at home, any high quality fruit preserve may be substituted for the House-Made Grape Jelly. This recipe, and its baking time and temperature, is specifically geared to our restaurant, which sits at 8,000 feet. You may need to experiment a little with the time and temperature.

320
Guest
Ranch

205 Buffalo Horn Creek
Highway 191, Mile Marker 36,
Big Sky, Montana

Reservations recommended

1-800-243-0320 or 406-995-4283
Open seasonally
Hours 5:30 to 9:00 pm
Website: www.320ranch.com

320 Guest Ranch

David Brask, Owner
Pat Sage, General Manager
Jeff Tappero, Chef

Deep in the heart of the Gallatin National Forest, the 320 Guest Ranch is located just minutes from Yellowstone National Park and Big Sky Ski Resort, with two miles of the renowned Gallatin River running through the property.

The 320 Guest Ranch and Resort offers a large variety of activities during the winter and summer months. In winter, the 320 Ranch features starlit sleigh rides to the Mountain Man Campsite, snowmobile excursions into Yellowstone Park, and Montana meals in the cozy restaurant complete with rock fireplace. In addition, the surrounding area offers some of the best backcountry snowmobiling and skiing—downhill, cross-country, and backcountry—to be found anywhere in the Rockies. For those interested in Yellowstone Park, the 320 is just 36 miles away, and snowmobile or snow coach trips can be arranged. Hike on snowshoes through deep powder for a truly exhilarating workout. Relax as a team of sled dogs pulls you along, yipping in excitement.

The 320 Ranch is also located near some of the best hunting in the world—from big game like elk, moose, and deer to ducks and grouse. They offer special hunting-season rates you won't find anywhere else.

The ranch comes alive in the summer with lots of fun outdoor activities and a true Western experience. Take a trail ride through the Gallatin National Forest with the ranch's wranglers, hike forest trails, fish in blue-ribbon trout streams, or sit on your front porch and enjoy the breathtaking scenery. Montana summers provide many adventures: historic ghost towns to be explored, whitewater rafting, mountain biking tours, rock climbing, tours of Yellowstone Park or a guided hike—the list of activities seems endless.

The 320 Guest Ranch launched into a stunning historical journey in the year 1898 when Sam Wilson homesteaded 160 acres along

A bird's-eye view of the 320 Ranch in Gallatin Canyon.

the Gallatin River. In 1900, Sam's father, Clinton, claimed an adjoining 160 acres and they combined the two properties and named the consolidated parcel the Buffalo Horn Resort. The original homestead cabin is still an important part of the 320 Guest Ranch and has been preserved as a part of the restaurant.

In 1904 employees of the Cooper Tie Logging Company constructed several cabins on the ranch in exchange for lodging. They worked the nearby Taylor Fork drainage, preparing timber for use as railroad ties. When the logging company went out of business in 1906, the Eldridge Post Office building was moved to the ranch and continued operating from there until it closed in 1938.

Dr. Caroline McGill

On January 16, 1936, Dr. Caroline McGill, a woman far ahead of her time, purchased the ranch from Mrs. Wilson. Montana's first woman doctor and first pathologist, Dr. McGill was an avid hunter and fisher. She believed that enjoying the outdoors was beneficial and bought the ranch as a place for her patients and friends to come to relax.

In 1938, Dr. McGill purchased a Cadillac engine in Idaho Falls that a friend, Jim Flint, installed to generate power. The ranch had power 10 years before power lines came into Gallatin Canyon.

Dinnertime at the 320 Ranch in the 1940s.

The ranch crew decided to build Dr. McGill a cabin closer to the office due to her advancing age. Finished on Christmas, it is known as the Christmas Cabin. She passed away in 1959. In her will, she gave the Goodrich family the option to purchase the 320 Guest Ranch. The family did buy the ranch and continued to run it as a guest ranch until 1987 when the current owner, Dave Brask, purchased it.

Under the ownership of Mr. Brask, the 320 Guest Ranch has grown from a capacity of 20 guests to well over 200. In the process, Mr. Brask has preserved all of the buildings that could be saved. The original homestead cabin is now a part of the 320 Steakhouse, containing antiques that Dave has purchased in his travels. He had Dr. McGill's original ranch house moved from the middle of the front pasture to a more peaceful setting near Buffalo Horn Creek.

The Christmas Cabin still remains and is occupied by 320 Ranch staff. Very few of the original buildings could be saved, but Dave has captured the feel of Montana with all of the new cabins and homes built of logs. Dave Brask enjoys the outdoors and believes in keeping the 320 Guest Ranch diverse in its operation and preserving the authenticity of the ranch atmosphere.

HALF BACON-WRAPPED PHEASANT
with a Merlot Honey Butter

Ingredients

3   2-pound pheasants, cut in quarters   Salt and pepper

24   pieces of bacon

Sauce

½   bottle merlot wine   2   teaspoon honey

1   medium shallot, finely diced   1   tablespoon butter

2   cloves garlic, finely diced

PREHEAT oven to 300°F.

SEASON the pheasant pieces and wrap each quarter with two pieces of bacon. Cook the bacon-wrapped pheasant on a sheet pan in the oven for 15-20 minutes.

IN A SAUCEPAN, add the shallots, garlic, and wine. Over low heat, reduce by three-fourths. Strain the garlic and shallots. Return to a simmer and add honey. Slowly add the butter, stirring constantly. Spoon the sauce over the pheasant and serve.

Serves 6

A couple enjoys an intimate evening at the 320 Ranch.

WAPITI PICATA

Ingredients

3   2-ounce wapiti (elk) tenderloin medallions

¼   cup flour

1   teaspoon shallots, finely diced

1   tablespoons capers, with juice

½   lemon

¼   cup heavy cream

    Salt and pepper

SEASON the flour to taste. Lightly coat the elk with flour. Preheat the oil in a sauté pan over medium heat. Lightly sear each side of the elk, approximately 2 minutes. Add the shallots and capers with juice. Slice one slice of lemon and set aside for garnish. Squeeze the juice from the remaining lemon and add to the pan. Reduce the heat to simmer and add the cream. Reduce by one half and serve immediately. Butterfly the lemon slice for garnish.

Serves 1

CAST-IRON TROUT
with Fresh Herbs and Lemon

Ingredients

½   cup flour

1   8-ounce trout butterflied with bones removed

½   lemon

1   teaspoon fresh thyme, finely chopped

1   teaspoon fresh rosemary, finely chopped

1   tablespoon butter

    Salt and pepper to taste

PREHEAT a cast-iron skillet over medium heat. Season the flour with salt and pepper. Lightly flour the trout. Add the butter to the skillet. Place the trout in the skillet skin side up. Cook until lightly browned and turn over. Slice a piece of lemon for garnish. Take a pinch of herbs and sprinkle over the trout. Squeeze the rest of the lemon juice over the trout, garnish and serve.

Serves 1

320 Berry Cobbler

Ingredients

4 cups Bisquick	7 cups fresh or frozen berries
1 cup milk	¾ cup granulated sugar
¼ cup rum	Cornstarch (as needed)
½ cup powdered sugar	

PREHEAT oven to 350°F.

MIX Bisquick, milk, rum, and powdered sugar. Put in cast-iron pot. Bake at 350°F until toothpick comes out dry. Let cool. Tip pot upside down and let breading fall out. Replace with berries and granulated sugar. Bring to a boil and add cornstarch until thick.

DROP breading on top and sprinkle with additional powdered sugar.

Serves 8–10

*Good things have been cooking in the
320 Ranch kitchen since the early 1900s.*

Healing Waters Lodge

270 Tuke Lane
Twin Bridges, Montana
406-684-5960

Open April to November
to Healing Waters guests
www.flyfishing-inn-montana.com

Healing Waters Lodge

Greg & Janet Lilly
Janet Lilly, Chef

Healing Waters Lodge was originally a small stone hospital built in 1895 in Sheridan, Montana. As with many old structures, the uses changed through the years, and in 1996 Greg and Janet Lilly bought what had been a private residence and converted it into one of the premier fly-fishing lodges in Montana.

Some of the special features of Healing Waters Lodge include two queen beds in each guest room (seven rooms total), fluffy down comforters and down pillows, private decks and patios for each guest room, mountain views from each room, private baths, and art and antiques that reflect the history of southwest Montana.

Healing Waters Lodge is centrally located amid southwest Montana's finest fishing. Each day you have the choice of fishing the Big Hole, Beaverhead, Ruby, Madison, or Jefferson Rivers. Float-fish the larger rivers and wade-fish the smaller meadow and mountain streams. Those anglers who enjoy stillwater fishing will find the Ruby Reservoir and Clark Canyon Reservoir to be as fine as any lakes in the country. Anglers travel from all over the world to enjoy the unmatched stream fishing available in southwest Montana.

Another amenity that Healing Waters provides for the non-angler in the party is an incomparable tour of the area sites; you'll see Montana's natural treasures in a way you never have, tailoring the activities of a day to appeal to your interests. You might hike and photograph wildflowers, wildlife, and the beautiful scenery of southwest Montana. Another day might be spent digging for quartz crystals, bird watching, or taking a relaxing dip in natural hot springs. Yet another choice is to visit nearby pioneer ghost towns like Virginia City and Nevada City and soak up the fascinating history of Montana's gold rush years. You can visit historical battlefields such as the Big Hole Battlefield where Chief Joseph gave the U.S. Army a lesson in guerrilla warfare. Healing Waters has guides exceptionally knowledgeable about Montana history from the time of Lewis and Clark's exploration through the war of the Copper Kings.

When you combine the wonderful ambiance of the lodge, built of native stone, handhewn logs, and Pennsylvania hardwoods, the indescribable meals, and experienced, professional fishing guides and naturalists, you get an experience that "heals your soul."

Black Bean Soup
with Cilantro Lime Sour Cream

Ingredients

1	16-ounce package dried black beans	2	tablespoons minced garlic
6	bacon slices, chopped	1	jalapeño chili, minced
¾	cup finely chopped celery	1	tablespoon red wine vinegar
¾	finely chopped onion	2	teaspoons ground cumin
¾	cup finely chopped carrots	1	teaspoon ground coriander
¾	cup finely chopped leeks	¾	cup sour cream
10	cups chicken broth	2	teaspoons fresh lemon juice
1	large tomato, chopped	2	teaspoons fresh lime juice
1	cup (packed) chopped fresh cilantro		Additional chopped fresh cilantro
3	cup (packed) chopped fresh parsley		Additional chopped tomato

Preparation

PLACE beans in large bowl. Add enough water to cover by 3 inches. Let stand overnight. Drain well. Cook bacon in heavy stockpot over medium heat until brown but still soft. Add celery, onion, carrots, and leeks and sauté until vegetables begin to soften. Add beans, chicken broth, tomato, ½ cup cilantro, parsley, garlic, jalapeno, vinegar, cumin, and coriander. Bring to boil. Reduce heat to medium low, cover, and simmer soup until beans are very tender, stirring occasionally, about 2 hours.

WORKING in batches, transfer all or part of soup to blender and process until slightly chunky purée forms. Return soup to pot. Season to taste with salt and pepper. Mix sour cream, lemon juice, lime juice, and ½ cup cilantro in small bowl. Ladle soup into bowls.

PLACE dollop of sour cream mixture atop soup. Garnish with additional chopped cilantro and chopped tomato.

Serves 8

Onion Tartlets with Crème Fraîche

Ingredients

3   tablespoons butter
1   package frozen puff pastry, thawed
2½ cups finely chopped onions

3   tablespoons water
½   cup crème fraîche or sour cream
2   tablespoons chopped fresh chives

Preparation

MELT butter in large skillet over medium heat. Add onions and cook until very tender and pale golden, stirring often and if necessary adding water to moisten. Cool. Preheat oven to 375°F. Roll out each pastry sheet on lightly floured surface to 12-inch square. Pierce pastry all over with fork. Using ½-inch diameter cookie cutter, cut out 18 rounds from each square. Place rounds on heavy baking sheets. Chill 15 minutes. Stir half of the crème fraîche into onion mixture. Season with salt and pepper. Spoon 1½ teaspoons onion mixture atop puff pastry round, flattening slightly with back of spoon. Bake until golden, about 25 minutes. (Can be made 2 hours ahead. Let stand at room temperature. Rewarm in 375°F oven until heated through.) Top with crème fraîche and chopped chives.

Makes 18

Jicama, Mango, and Watercress Salad

Dressing

¾ cup walnut oil
6 tablespoons white wine vinegar

5 tablespoons chopped cilantro
3 tablespoons toasted pecans

WHISK walnut oil, vinegar, and cilantro in small bowl. Stir in pecans and season with salt and pepper.

Salad

2 large bunches watercress
2 small red bell peppers (matchstick strips)

2 cups jicama (matchstick strips)
2 cups fresh mangos (matchstick strips)
½ cup pecan halves, toasted

COMBINE all vegetables and toss with dressing to coat. Sprinkle with pecans and serve.

Serves 8

BABY BACK PORK RIBS
with Guava Barbecue Sauce

Ingredients

4	cups water		4	teaspoons ground black pepper
3	cups chopped onions		1	tablespoon salt
¾	cup red wine vinegar		4	bay leaves
½	cup chopped fresh cilantro		3	tablespoon chopped garlic
6	tablespoons chopped fresh oregano		7-7½	pounds baby pork back ribs, cut into 7 rib pieces
4	teaspoons cumin			

MIX 4 cups water, onions, vinegar, cilantro, oregano, garlic, cumin, pepper, salt, and bay leaves in large bowl. Place rib sections, rounded side down, in two roasting pans. Pour marinade over ribs. Cover and chill overnight, occasionally basting.

PREHEAT oven to 500°F.

ROAST ribs uncovered in marinade until cooked through, about 35 minutes. Cool slightly.

PREPARE barbecue grill or maintain oven temperature at 500°F. Remove ribs from marinade and discard remaining marinade. Sprinkle ribs with salt and pepper. Cut ¼-inch deep incisions between ribs (do not cut through) to allow Guava Barbecue Sauce to permeate meat.

BRUSH ribs with Guava Barbecue Sauce. Grill or bake ribs until well browned, basting often with more sauce, about 6 minutes per side. Cut into individual ribs and serve.

For the Guava Barbecue Sauce

2	11½-ounce cans guava nectar		1½	tablespoons chopped garlic
3	tablespoons red wine vinegar		⅓	cup sherry
1½	cups chopped onions		1	tablespoons ground cumin
2	tablespoons tomato paste		¼	cup light molasses
¾	cup guava jelly or red currant jelly		2	teaspoons dry mustard

WHISK all ingredients in large saucepan. Boil mixture, whisking until jelly dissolves. Reduce heat and simmer until sauce is reduced to 3 cups. Cool.

Serves 6

Mango Mousse

Ingredients

28   ounces fresh or canned mangos
1   can condensed milk
½   cup fresh lime juice

¼   cup whipping cream, whipped
Fresh mint leaves

PLACE mangos, condensed milk, and lime juice into blender. Process until well-blended. Pour into eight individual bowls or goblets. Chill. Serve with whipped cream and mint leaves or diced kiwi fruit and mango.

Serves 8

Fresh Lime-Coconut Pie
with Macadamia-Coconut Crust

Ingredients

35   vanilla wafer cookies
⅓   cup dry roasted macadamia nuts
⅓   cup sweetened flaked coconut
¼   cup unsalted butter, melted
1   15-ounce can cream of coconut
⅔   cup plain yogurt
½   cup fresh lime juice

2   teaspoons lime zest
3   tablespoons cold water
2   teaspoons unflavored gelatin
¾   cup chilled whipping cream, whipped
2   tablespoons confectioners' sugar
1   lime, thinly sliced into rounds
Additional confectioners' sugar

For the Crust

PREHEAT oven to 350°F.

FINELY grind cookies and nuts in processor. Transfer to bowl. Mix in coconut. Add butter and stir until blended. Press crumb mixture into bottom and sides of 9-inch glass pie plate. Cover and freeze 30 minutes, then bake 20 minutes until golden. Cool well.

For the Filling

WHISK cream of coconut, yogurt and lime juice and zest in large bowl. Pour the 3 table-spoons cold water into small metal bowl. Sprinkle gelatin over. Let stand 10 minutes. Set bowl in small saucepan of simmering water, whisk until gelatin dissolves. Whisk into coconut mixture. Pour into crust. Chill until set, about 4 hours or overnight. Beat cream and confectioners' sugar until soft peaks form. Transfer to pastry bag with large star tip. Pipe around edges of pie. Dip lime slices in additional powdered sugar. Garnish pie with lime.

Serves 6-8

The Continental Divide

East Main Street
Ennis, Montana
406-682-7600

Open for Dinner
May 1 to Mid-October
Hours: 6:00 to 10:00 pm

The Continental Divide

Eric and Marzena Trapp, Owners
Eric Trapp, Chef

The Continental Divide was opened in the summer of 1982 by Jay and Karen Bentley and was acquired by Eric and Marzena Trapp in 1999. It began as a small, seasonal fine-dining restaurant catering mostly to the fly-fishing enthusiasts that visit Montana each year. French and Creole cuisine was the culinary theme, emphasizing an experience that was difficult to find elsewhere in Montana at the time. Seating only 30-40 people depending on weather, casual elegance, and quality helped the business to develop an outstanding reputation. The Continental Divide has been reviewed by *The New York Times*, *Esquire Magazine*, *House & Garden*, *Big Sky Journal*, *Bugle Magazine*, and continues to get consistently rave reviews.

The new owners, recognizing that fine cuisine in Montana is no longer rare, are committed to providing fine food paired with excellent wines in a relaxing dining experience. Local organic produce and free range poultry, local wild mushrooms, only wild fresh fish, exotic game, aged U.S.D.A Prime beef, all are painstakingly sought after and carefully prepared. Although small, the wine list is designed not only to match the cuisine but to offer many boutique selections as well as familiar favorites. The Continental Divide opens the first of May and is open until mid-October every summer for dinner only. From July 4th weekend to Labor Day there is also a "Live" Jazz Sunday brunch weather permitting. Dining at the Continental Divide is summed up by their motto "EAT, MEET, & FISH."

The Lapin á la Moutarde.

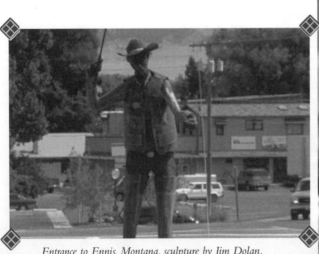

Entrance to Ennis, Montana, sculpture by Jim Dolan.

Lapin á la Moutarde
(Rabbit with Mustard)

People often steer away from eating rabbit because of its well deserved reputation for being dry. This method is my favorite for many meats, but especially for rabbit.

Ingredients

1 rabbit per every three or four people, cut into even pieces (6-8 pieces per rabbit depending on the size)

Lots of rendered duck fat (may substitute with an oil, but try not to)

Curing spice rub; for rabbit I use fresh thyme, rosemary, sage, dried red chile, black pepper, and salt

MIX TO YOUR taste, but not too much salt, sage, or red pepper, as they overwhelm.

Sauce

⅓ cup Dijon mustard

½ cup white wine

1 tablespoon fresh shallots

1 tablespoon fresh garlic

2 tablespoons crème fraîche

White pepper

Method for the Sauce *(Keeps a few days)*

SWEAT minced shallots and garlic in a heavy saucepan, and before they brown, add mustard. Stir constantly for about half a minute to mellow the mustard and add wine. Reduce by one-third. Add crème fraîche, simmer a few minutes, add a pinch of white pepper, and strain through a fine sieve. Reserve in a squeeze bottle. (If you can't buy crème fraîche make your own. To a quart of heavy fresh cream, add ¼ cup of buttermilk and let sit in a warm spot [65-80°F] until it sets up and then refrigerate.)

RUB the rabbit pieces generously with spice mix and reserve in a steel or glass pan. Overnight is best, 8-12 hours. Take cured pieces and lightly brush them off with your hands, leave a thin layer on the rabbit. Place rabbit in a large baking dish and completely submerge in rendered duck fat. Then place in a 200-220°F oven for 4-7 hours until the meat wants to fall from the bone; but doesn't quite. Gently place the rabbit on a draining rack (a cake cooling rack works great). At this point you can refrigerate the rabbit and reheat later in the oven at medium heat, or serve right away.

I like to serve this with Israeli Couscous and roasted vegetables, but many combinations work well. Arrange the rabbit on plates with side dishes and "paint" it with the sauce from the squeeze bottle. A trick to this is to hold the bottle high and work quickly, not trying to be perfect but to have fun with it. I think this dish demands a nice red burgundy wine—a good Croze-Hermitage or Cote D'Beaune at least.

MACADAMIA-CRUSTED ONO (WAHOO)

*with Fresh Chive Oil, Truffled Jasmine Rice,
and Steamed Vegetables*

One of the best surprises for travelers and locals in Montana is fresh fish. That's right, we are only a few hours from Seattle by air, and fresh seafood is flown to Montana at least three days a week, if not more, in the busy season. This allows the Continental Divide and others to offer seafood and shellfish 1-2 days from catch to table when conditions permit. This recipe works with any boned white-fleshed fish, but when fresh Ono is available it is my first choice. If you can get fresh Ono, please be gentle. It's tragic to overcook this fish. Make sure your guests are seated and comfortable before cooking. A dry Riesling from Alsace (France) or Piesporter (Germany) complements the textures of this dish, or, of course, a full-bodied Chardonnay, not too heavy with oak, would suffice.

Ingredients

7	ounce pieces fresh-skinned and boned Ono (Wahoo)
½	ounce (per person) macadamia nuts, (preferably not roasted)
½	ounce (per person) Japanese Panko bread crumbs
1	cup fresh heavy cream
3	bunches fresh chives

1 ½   cups good olive oil

¼   cup (per person) Jasmine rice

Good quality truffled olive oil

Truffle peelings, if available

Shredded fresh carrots, fresh snap, or snow peas

Butter, optional

Cheesecloth

Method

ROUGHLY grate the macadamia nuts. I use the cheese-grating blade of my Cuisinart. Don't worry if it is messy or incomplete. Leave the nuts in the bowl and add about two-thirds of the bread crumbs. If the nuts are unsalted, add a pinch or two of salt. Change to the chopping blade and pulse the two ingredients together without overprocessing. Two or three times is enough. The Panko adds texture, color, and is lighter than pure nuts. Reserve mixture to a large bowl. Put the olive oil into a good blender; then wash chives and toss into a hot sauté pan with a touch of oil; toss a few times and then into the blender. You could also blanch them in boiling water, then chill and add, but I like the flavor more with the sauté. Blend the oil and sautéed chives, about 45 seconds depending on the strength of your machine. Don't overprocess or there will be sediment in the finished product. Either leave in the blender for a few hours or transfer to a non-transparent container for 3-4 hours. Then strain through cheesecloth. This oil can be kept covered in a cool dark place for a day or two before the chlorophyll begins to decay.

OIL should be bright green and quite aromatic. Cook the jasmine rice according to instructions, but only use plain water, and halfway through throw in a small amount of truffle peelings. When cooked, transfer to a large mixing bowl and very gently fold in truffle oil to taste, a little salt and white pepper, and if desired, some melted butter. Rub or spray some olive oil into a coffee cup per person and fill firmly with rice. If serving right away place on serving plate upside down, tap, and unmold. If waiting, cover with plastic wrap and gently microwave (that's right) a few minutes before service and let rest before unmolding on plates.

DIP non-skin side of fish into fresh cream, then press into macadamia mixture (one side only). Gently pick it up and firmly press the mixture into the fish with the palm of your hand. Then place the macadamia side down into an oiled warm (not smoking hot) sauté pan, and turn up flame. When nuts are just golden, take out the fish and place in a baking dish, nuts up, and then into a 350-400°F oven until almost flaking; 5-10 minutes depending on the oven and how much is in it. If the oven is too hot the nuts will burn, if too cold the fish loses texture. Ono is a firm fish and when done to flaking, it is overdone. It should have lost that "wiggly" feeling in the middle and the edges should want to flake.

UNMOLD the rice, and with a large spatula place the fish firmly into the rice so it is above plate level but not actually stacked, then decorate with fresh steamed shredded carrots and peas tossed in either butter or chive oil and lightly season with salt and pepper. Then drizzle with chive oil, making sure there is at least one area of the plate with a little drizzle of bright green visible.

Serves 1

Broiled Foie Gras with Tobikko Caviar (recipe follows).

Broiled Foie Gras with Tobikko Caviar
on Roasted Garlic Toast

I love appetizers! Even though they can be time-consuming to prepare, and often a very high-cost food item, the Continental Divide always offers an interesting array. Guests often join us just for these items and a nice glass of wine. This classicly simple recipe is rarely on the menu, and was created expressly for the birthday of one of our favorite people. Her husband rented the entire restaurant and invited many of the local fishing guides and restaurant regulars. It is easy to make, and has gorgeous contrast. Pair with a crisp, flinty Chardonnay; Neyers Reserve, Les Pierres from Sonoma Cutrer, or your favorite 1st Cru French Chablis.

Ingredients

- 3 ounces (per person) fresh foie gras, a good grade B + will do nicely.
- ½ ounce (per person) fresh Orange Tobikko
- 2 slices (per person) bread for toasting, allow for mistakes. (I prefer "English Muffin Toasting Bread" in the Blue and White wrapper.) But any white sliced bread will suffice.

Roasted Garlic Oil, I make my own by simmering peeled garlic cloves in good olive oil, but you don't have to.

Method

FIRST cut crusts off of the bread. Then cut four points per slice: Cut from right bottom corner to the middle of the opposite side, repeat from left side, then from point of remaining piece cut in half. This should create four identical long pointy triangles. Brush lightly with garlic oil and toast under broiler until golden brown and crunchy. Don't over-oil them as the Foie Gras is already rich. This can be done a few hours ahead, but leave uncovered so they stay dry.

CAREFULLY pull any veins and connective tissue from the Foie Gras and slice into fairly regular ¼-inch slices. Pull any remaining veins as you go. Reserve Foie Gras on a baking sheet with four sides (to prevent oil spillage). One trick is to make sure the Foie Gras is very cold, but not frozen, to facilitate slicing. Cut any very big pieces down to fit on the toast points. This doesn't have to be exact. Open the Tobikko and get a small plastic or glass spoon to handle it.

NEXT, decorate your serving platter or appetizer plate. I like something minimalistic but decadent to reflect the nature of the dish. Little edible viola flowers or a squash blossom for example. Place the Foie Gras under a hot broiler until reduced in size (roughly one-fourth to one-fifth). There will be loads of rendered fat left. You should save this for other uses. With tongs, very gently lay the pieces on the toast points, combining if needed to cover them at least by two-thirds. This is the trickiest part. Don't break the points or crush the Foie Gras. Next balance a generous spoon of Tobikko on top of every piece and arrange on the platter or dish. The neon of the Tobikko, the smooth richness of the Foie Gras, and the crisp crunch of the garlic toasts, followed by the lingering popping of the Tobikko will delight even your guests who say they "hate liver." Be sure to make more than you think you'll need.

Potosi Hot Springs Resort

1 South Willow Creek Road
6½ miles south of Pony, Montana
Open year-round, 7 days a week,
24 hours a day

Hot springs and other facilities are
for overnight guests only.

The restaurant is open for dinner
to the public for groups of 8 or
more *(advance reservation required)*

406-685-3330 or 1-888-685-1695
www.potosiresort.com

Potosi
Hot Springs

Nick Kern & Christine Stark,
Owners
Christine Stark, Chef

The area where Potosi Hot Springs Resort is located has a wild history. There are tipi rings in the area, evidence that this region was originally occupied at times by Native American tribes who surely enjoyed the healing properties and comfort of the hot springs as much as we do. There is even evidence that these mountains were mined as far back as the 1600s by Spanish explorers. However, the modern history of Potosi dates back to the late 1800s when the area was developing as a gold mining hot-bed. Virginia City was the state capital at that time, and Butte was the biggest city in the territory. Pony at one time had a population of about 2,000-4,000 people, whereas today there are only about 75 year-round residents. Eventually President Taft signed the Placer Mining Claims that currently make up the property of Potosi Hot Springs Resort.

This 75-acre inholding in the Beaverhead-Deerlodge National Forest was set off primarily to become a resort, with the focus on the hot springs. There was a 14-room lodge built in the 1880s on the same site as the current main lodge. This beautiful old hotel and restaurant was accessed by cart and buggy only. The owner would drive down the 6½-mile dirt road and pick up guests at the train line that spurred off from Harrison and came into Pony. This remote lodge prospered for a number of years until it was sold in the 1930s or '40s to a local rancher who moved the structure to his ranch. The building was later sold off for lumber. From the day that the hotel was removed, the area became a public place for camping, picnicking, and enjoying the hot spring pool that had been built in 1892. The area remained this way until the 1960s.

At some point the canyon became the home to a "hippie commune." They apparently moved in and settled in the canyon past the springs. The locals felt they had lost their spot, and in order to get the group to leave, blew up the walls of the pool with dynamite. Needless to say, this worked and the commune left.

In the mid-1970s Pete and Virginia Gross purchased the property and built a residence that is now the main lodge. They lived here for about 10 years as

Potosi Hot Springs, Pony

88

they developed another hot spring and rebuilt the walls to the pool (the floor of the pool is still the original floor poured in 1892). They eventually sold the property to the Trapp family, who lived in the residence for four years before deciding to build the four cabins and make a business out of it.

On April 7, 2000 Nick Kern and Christine Stark became the new owners of this truly amazing property. Since the purchase they have made a number of improvements, including a new hot springs and a sauna. They have also managed to build a strong, steady business, which has gained national media attention as well as a fantastic "word of mouth" reputation. This is the history of Potosi thus far, and hopefully the future history will be just as entertaining.

The updated Potosi Hot Springs Resort combines mountain seclusion with luxury accommodations and excellent gourmet, Western cuisine, providing the ultimate Montana escape.

Potosi offers guests a wide variety or activities year-round. Guided fly-fishing trips, horsepack trips, nature hikes, historic tours, mountain biking, whitewater rafting, and many other outdoor adventures are all available through the resort. In the fall, the guided hunting opportunities are abundant. In the winter, Potosi Hot Springs Resort offers a pristine playground for snowshoeing, cross-country skiing, and backcountry skiing/snowboarding expeditions to the high alpine peaks that surround Potosi. Any time of year is an ideal time to stay at Potosi Hot Springs Resort.

The Potosi Hotel before 1918.

ROASTED QUAIL
with Cranberry Compote

For the Quail

8	cleaned small whole quails, wing tips clipped
4	cloves garlic
1	bunch fresh rosemary

1	orange, cut into small sections
	Olive oil
	Salt and pepper
	Kitchen string

For the Compote

1	liter port wine
1½	cups fresh cranberries
1	cup water
1	cup sugar
2	sprigs fresh rosemary
1	teaspoon cinnamon

½	teaspoon ground cloves
	Grated fresh nutmeg, or ½ teaspoon ground nutmeg
1	tablespoon orange zest
3	tablespoons Grand Marnier

Preparation

PREHEAT oven to 375°F.

CUT garlic cloves in half and place halves into each quail cavity along with a sprig of rosemary and an orange section. Brush quail body with olive oil and rub salt and pepper into skin. Using kitchen string, tie legs and wrap around and under wings. Tie off to hold, and set into shallow baking dish. Cover lightly, and set aside.

POUR port wine into saucepan and slowly bring to light boil. Allow port to reduce by about half. In another small saucepan, combine cranberries, water, sugar, spices, and rosemary and bring to a light boil. Cook about 10 minutes, or until all cranberries have popped and liquid is deep red. Carefully remove rosemary. Add cranberry mixture to port wine reduction in small spoonfuls. Simmer while quail are roasting. Roast quail (uncovered) at 375°F for 3 minutes, then turn oven down to 325°F. Roast another 10-12 minutes or until meat thermometer registers 170°F. Remove from oven and lightly cover. Add orange zest and Grand Marnier to port-cranberry sauce. Just before serving, spoon sauce over quail (after removing kitchen string and garlic/rosemary/orange) and serve two quails per person. Garnish with fresh rosemary and a twist of orange.

THIS dish is wonderful with wild rice or mashed potatoes. You may want to substitute quail for the traditional holiday turkey, or serve them at a winter dinner party. Asparagus, sugar snap peas, even brussels sprouts go well with quail. You can also try this compote on pheasant or other game birds, although it is not recommended with duck or goose.

POTOSI'S POACHED TROUT

For the Trout

3	whole rainbow trout
2	cups white wine
6	tablespoons unsalted butter, cut into ¼ -inch pieces
6	sprigs fresh dill
	Salt and pepper

Two lemons, one thinly sliced, one for garnish

Cooking spray

Aluminum foil: 6 sheets, about 12 inches square

Preparation

PREHEAT oven to 350°F.

PLACE two pieces of foil on top of each other, roll edges together on one side, and open the foil pieces like a book. Spray the inside of the foil with cooking spray and set aside, with rolled edge facing away. Using a very sharp knife, remove the head just behind the gills, and slice the trout into two filets, along the backbone and through the tail. Trim the fins off the body. Rinse well under cold water and pat dry with paper towels. Place each trout filet skin side down on foil. Top with butter pieces, dill sprig, and 3-4 lemon slices. Sprinkle salt and pepper on top. Slightly fold edges of foil upwards, and carefully pour about ½ cup of white wine into the packet. Roll the remaining three edges of foil packet together, and cut a slit into the top to allow for steam release during the cooking process. Repeat this process for remaining filets. These packets can be cooked on a grill over medium heat about 8-10 min-utes or on a tray in your oven at about 350°F for 8-10 minutes. Be careful letting steam escape when opening the cooked trout packets!

To serve

REMOVE the cooked lemons and dill, then replace the lemon slices on top of the filets when ready to serve.

RISOTTO, a fresh green salad, roasted potatoes, grilled veggies or corn-on-the-cob are delicious with this dish. The options are endless!

Serves 6

MIXED GREENS
WITH BLUEBERRIES, SHAVED FENNEL
AND CHÈVRE ROUNDS
with Potosi's Balsamic Vinaigrette

Ingredients for the Salad

5-6 cups of fresh salad greens (mixed spring greens or mesclun mix)

1 pint fresh blueberries

1 fresh fennel bulb, stalks trimmed

1 large roll of chèvre cheese (can be found in most grocery stores)

2 tablespoons ground black pepper

For the Potosi Vinaigrette

½ cup balsamic vinegar

2 tablespoons port wine

1 teaspoon white granulated sugar

1 teaspoon minced shallot

1 teaspoon fresh mint, julienne

1 cup extra virgin olive oil

Preparation

ADD the dressing ingredients to a bowl or salad dressing shaker, whisk or shake well. Refrigerate until ready to use, then bring to room temperature before dressing the greens. Dressing will keep for a week refrigerated.

RINSE greens and place into a large bowl. Drizzle 4-6 tablespoons (to taste) of the dressing over the greens and lightly toss. Arrange about 1½ cups of dressed greens per serving on small plates (or 3 cups per entrée on two large plates). Sprinkle about 1-2 tablespoons blueberries over the greens. Using a mandoline or a very sharp knife, carefully slice the fennel bulb crosswise. Arrange shaved fennel slices on top of the greens and berries. Slice chèvre crosswise into ¼- to ½-inch slices. Put pepper in a flat dish, and roll the edges of the chèvre rounds in the pepper. (Allow two rounds per serving.) Arrange rounds over the greens and serve.

IF SERVING as an entrée, top salad with grilled chicken or fish, then arrange berries, fennel, and chèvre.

Serves 4-6, as a starter course
Serves 2 as an entrée topped with grilled chicken or fish

COUNTRY POTATOES
with Scallions

Ingredients

2   pounds small to medium red potatoes

2   cups heavy cream

5   tablespoons unsalted butter
    Salt and freshly ground pepper to
    taste

2   bunches scallions (green onions)
    including greens, washed, trimmed,
    and diagonally sliced

Preparation

WASH and dice potatoes, leaving skin on. Add to pot, cover with cold water, and bring to a boil. Cook for about 15-20 minutes, or until potatoes are tender. Drain water, add 4 table-spoons butter to potatoes in the pot, cover and set aside. In skillet, melt remaining butter and add scallions. Season with salt and pepper and allow to cook 4-5 minutes, until onions are tender but still bright green. Add cooked scallions to potatoes, add cream, and mash using a hand masher until large potato pieces are mashed but not completely smooth. Add salt and pepper to taste, and more cream if desired to reach the preferred consistency.

Serves 4-6

BROWN SUGAR GLAZED FRENCH BEANS

Ingredients

2   pounds French beans (haricot vert) or
    thin green beans, washed with stem
    ends trimmed

2   tablespoons unsalted butter

3   tablespoons brown sugar

¼   cup water
    Salt to taste

HEAT nonstick skillet over medium flame, add butter and allow to melt. Turn down heat if butter starts to turn brown. Add beans and toss to coat with butter. Cover pan and cook for 2 minutes. Lift cover carefully to avoid steam, add water and brown sugar and toss to coat. Cover pan and cook an additional 3-4 minutes or until beans are bright green. Add salt to taste and serve immediately.

Serves 8-10

POTOSI'S LIME TART
with Chambord Cream and Berries

For the Crust

1	*package graham crackers*
½	*cup macadamia nuts, shelled and whole*

2	*tablespoons unsalted butter*
	10-inch tart pan with removable bottom

For the Filling

2	*teaspoons lime zest (use rasp or zester)*
	Juice of 8 large limes

6	*large eggs*
1½	*cups white sugar*
1	*cup unsalted butter*

For the Garnish

3	*cups heavy cream*
¼	*cup Chambord (raspberry liqueur)*
3	*tablespoons powdered sugar*

½	*pint fresh raspberries*
24	*pieces lime peel*

Preparation

PREHEAT oven to 325°F.

COMBINE graham crackers and macadamia nuts in food processor, and pulse into small crumbs. Melt 2 tablespoons butter in medium bowl in microwave, then add crumb mixture to melted butter. Stir with fork until crumbs are evenly moistened, and transfer crumb mixture to tart pan. Press crumb mixture into the sides of the pan, and firmly into the bottom. Bake at 325°F for about 10 minutes, or until crust is golden brown. Remove from oven and let cool.

COMBINE lime juice, 1 cup butter, and ½ cup sugar in saucepan. Melt mixture over very low heat, stirring occasionally. In separate bowl, add eggs, remaining sugar, and lime zest, and whisk until well blended. When saucepan mixture has melted, slowly add to egg mixture, whisking continually. Add this combined mixture back into saucepan, turn heat up to medium, and whisk continually until it slightly thickens, about 3-5 minutes. Remove from heat and gently pour mixture into tart pan. Put tart into refrigerator uncovered for about 2 hours. Then cover well with plastic wrap, and refrigerate another 4-6 hours before serving.

Presentation

WHIP the heavy cream, Chambord and powdered sugar in a bowl (or standing mixer) until thick. Place tart slice on small plate, spoon cream over, and arrange raspberries on the plate with lime peel.

Serves 10-12

PEAR AND PLUM TART
with Vanilla Bean and Thyme Glaze

For the Filling

10-12	Italian plums, firm
8	Bosc pears, firm
2	lemons, juice of
1	cup white sugar
1	tablespoon flour

1	cup thyme jelly (available at some supermarkets or from the Internet)
1	vanilla bean
1	sprig fresh thyme
¾	cup water

Special Equipment

10-inch tart pan with removable bottom

Preparation

PREHEAT oven to 350°F.

ROLL out pastry (see Potosi's Pastry Recipe page 96) to ¼-inch thickness to fit 10-inch tart pan. Gently drape pastry over pan and press into the sides and bottom. Remove overlapping pastry by pressing it against the edge of the pan all the way around. Place the tart pan in refrigerator until ready to fill the tart.

WASH, seed, and thinly slice pears. Place in bowl and add half the lemon juice, ¾ cup of white sugar, and flour. Toss gently and set aside. Wash plums and slice in half, removing the pits. Place in bowl and add remaining lemon juice and sugar. Toss gently and set aside.

IN SMALL saucepan, add thyme jelly, water, vanilla bean (halved lengthwise), and fresh thyme. Simmer for 15-20 minutes, do not boil. When slightly cooled, pour through a strainer into a small bowl.

ARRANGE pear slices in tart shell, fanning out from the center. Add plum halves to center of tart and around the edges, skin side up. Pour jelly mixture evenly over the entire tart. Place in 350°F oven for 30-40 minutes, checking frequently to make sure pastry does not over brown. Remove from oven and let cool. Serve slice of tart with fresh vanilla whipped cream or ice cream. Garnish with fresh thyme.

Serves 10-12

POTOSI'S PASTRY RECIPE

For the Pastry

2 cups white flour	2 teaspoons white sugar
½ cup (1 stick) cold unsalted butter, cut into ¼-inch dice	1 large egg, beaten lightly with 6 tablespoons cold water
Pinch sea salt	

Preparation

IN A large bowl combine flour, butter, salt, and sugar and crumble with fingers until it is the consistency of cornmeal. Form a depression in the mixture and add the egg and water. Mix with fork until it forms a messy ball, adding more flour if too wet. Divide in half and tightly wrap each half in plastic wrap. Label and place in freezer until ready to use.

WHEN ready to use, remove from freezer a couple hours prior to using the pastry. It's best to work with when very cold. Use frozen pastry within 30 days.

The massage tipi in summer..

Try a massage in the winter after a ski trip.

Jackson Hot Springs Lodge

JACKSON
HOT SPRINGS LODGE & RESORT

JACKSON IS MONTANA

Highway 278
Jackson, Montana
406-834-3151

Open 7 days a week, year-long

Friday and Saturday,
7:00 am to midnight

Sunday through Thursday,
7 am to 10 pm (when busy,
the lodge will stay open to
accommodate guests)

www.jacksonhotsprings.com
hotresort@jacksonhotsprings.com

Public hot springs; lodging available

Jackson Hot Springs Lodge

The Peterson Family, Owners
Boni Roberts & Anita Faust, Chefs

The tiny cow town at the end of the Big Hole Valley of southwest Montana was named for the town's first postmaster, Antone Jackson. On July 7, 1806, shortly after Lewis and Clark separated during their return from the Pacific Ocean, Clark discovered the hot springs in the Big Hole Valley (which he called "Hot Springs Valley"). Clark and his party, along with their Shoshone Indian guide Sacajawea, settled around the hot springs for their noonday lunch. At this time, Clark cooked a piece of meat "the width of two fingers" in the steaming water, noting that in five minutes the meat was cooked enough to eat and that the water "blubbers with heat for twenty paces below where it rises."

In 1884 Benoit O. Fournier made public claim to the springs where he built his home and a small plunge. Sometime in 1898 the local paper reported that "a bath in the hot water is one of the luxuries which people usually take advantage of when in town."

It was in 1911 that M. D. Jardine purchased the springs and built the first hotel on Main Street, along with a public plunge to which he piped the hot springs water 1,300 feet from its source. In 1950, the resort was purchased by John Dooling, a successful rancher from Jackson Hole, Wyoming. Dooling's dream was to construct a new log inn and hot springs pool, which he completed later that year. Originally named the Diamond Bar Inn, the new lodge cost Dooling approximately $400,000 and quickly became the center of activity of outdoor enthusiasts in the Big Hole Valley. Since the 1960s the lodge has gone through several owners and has been owned by the Peterson family since 1990.

Gleaming woodwork, polished floors, clean, bright hot pool open to the stars, spruced-up grounds, and congenial staff have turned the lodge into a community gathering spot.

*The comfortable lobby and dining area
of the Jackson Hot Springs Lodge.*

BUFFALO NEW YORK STRIP WITH CARAMELIZED GARLIC BUTTER SAUCE

Recipe by Boni Roberts

The first night we prepared this recipe, we sold out!

Ingredients

4   10- to 12-ounce buffalo New York strip steaks (can substitute any wild game or beef)
3   tablespoons butter

Steak Seasoning

2   tablespoons kosher salt or 1 tablespoon + 1 teaspoon table salt

1   tablespoon pepper (coarse ground black pepper if possible)

2   teaspoons garlic, granulated or powder

¼   teaspoon cayenne pepper

1   teaspoon granulated onion or onion powder

Caramelized Garlic Butter Sauce

½   cup thinly sliced garlic (slice thin by hand or use smallest blade on food processor)

2-4 tablespoons oil (vegetable or olive oil)

¼   teaspoon coarse black pepper or cracked black pepper

½   teaspoon salt

½   cup white wine

1   tablespoon Worcestershire sauce

¼   cup beef stock or beef broth

1   teaspoon granulated onion or powdered onion

½   cup butter (cut into pieces)

Cooking Instructions for the Steak

MIX dry steak seasonings together. Sprinkle over both sides of steaks. Let rest. Melt butter in heavy pan over medium heat. When butter begins to brown add seasoned steaks. Cook/brown on both sides 2 minutes. Remove from pan. Put in new pan, slightly buttered. Bake in oven until desired temperature of 350° to 400°F is reached, anywhere from 5 to 15 minutes. While steaks are in oven, make sauce.

For the Caramelized Garlic Butter Sauce

PUT OIL in heavy-bottomed pan, over medium heat. When oil is warm add sliced garlic. Sauté, stirring occasionally until golden brown. Add salt, pepper, and wine. Cook for two minutes at medium-high heat. Add beef stock or beef broth, Worcestershire, and granulated onion. Bring to boil then simmer for two minutes. Stir in a couple tablespoons of butter at a time. Stir until completely incorporated before adding additional butter. Repeat. Serve warm sauce over steaks.

Serves 4

FETA-SPINACH CHICKEN
Recipe by Nita Faust

This has turned out to be a delightful addition to our regular menu. We have presented this as a regular entrée since its creation about a year ago. Patrons, as well as staff, request this entrée often and wait patiently for it to be prepared. We prepare this dish per order, which takes 30 minutes bake time. The combination of flavors and the lightness of the dish makes for pure dining pleasure.

Ingredients (per 8-ounce breast)

Chicken breast, skinned and boneless, butterflied

Fresh feta cheese, crumbled (2 ounces)

Fresh spinach, 6-8 whole leaves

Panko bread crumbs

Dried thyme

Lemon juice, fresh or bottled

Butter, melted

Salt and pepper to taste

Preparation

PREHEAT oven to 450°F.

RINSE and pat dry individual chicken breast. Cut breast almost in half horizontally and lay open. Place 6 to 8 spinach leaves across center of split breast and then about 2 ounces of the crumbled feta. Starting at the thin end of the breast, roll the chicken around the spinach and feta. Then wrap chicken breast in plastic wrap for a couple of minutes. This helps the chicken stick to itself and keeps each roll beautiful for the next step.

COAT chicken by rolling the breast gently in a prepared dish of lemon juice and then rolling it in a prepared dish of Panko. Place breast on a baking tray, put a little extra Panko crumbs on top, drizzle with small amount of melted butter, and then a couple of dashes of thyme. Bake for 30 minutes.

For the Sauce

1   teaspoon of butter

1   tablespoon of lemon juice

   Dash of thyme

2   ounces 100% heavy whipping cream

   Salt and pepper (sort of like a sprinkle of each between your fingers)

Presentation

SPOON reduced sauce onto serving plate, cut baked chicken breast diagonally (as this gives the best presentation of the spinach and feta) and place on the sauce. Serve hot.

WE often prepare a number of chicken breasts to this point, in advance of serving time. You may also elect to freeze the chicken breasts now, especially if planning for a special function.

Serves 1

COWBOY BEEF FILET MIGNON
Recipe by Nita Faust

This entrée was introduced because we wanted a new finish to our filet that would be an enhancement but not overpowering to the meat. We are in beef country, and the distinction of our meats is defined at our dining tables. This dish is offered on our regular menu and continues to be a wonderful seller. Although it is not the nature of this chef to serve any meat "well done," this presentation works wonderfully for the most rare of steaks to the most thoroughly cooked.

Ingredients (per filet)

	Filet mignon	1	teaspoon garlic, chopped
2	tablespoons butter	1	dash Worcestershire sauce
2	mushrooms, sliced	2	ounces sweet vermouth
1	tablespoon shallots, chopped	2	ounces beef broth
1	tablespoon scallions, chopped		Salt and pepper, a good pinch of each

Preparation

ASK each guest how they would like their filet cooked and grill individual filets. Each filet is made to order and will be finished in the mushroom sauce.

Sauce

SAUTÉ mushrooms, shallots, scallions, and garlic in the butter. Add Worcestershire sauce, sweet vermouth, and beef broth and reduce. Place grilled filet into the sauce reduction, and turn at least once to finish. The sauce should be reduced by half when finished.

Presentation

PLACE filet on serving plate and pour sauce over the filet. The presentation of the natural pour of the sauce over the filet will delight anyone.

Serves 1

GARLIC PARMESAN BREAD
Recipe by Delila Dawson

We make our dinner breads each week. This is one of our most requested breads.

Ingredients

2 ½ teaspoons yeast, high altitude
(at lower altitude use ½ teaspoon
less yeast)

8 cups sugar

¾ cup evaporated milk

2 large eggs

½ teaspoon salt

¼ cup butter

2 tablespoons garlic, minced

1 cup freshly grated Parmesan cheese

6 cups flour (approximately)

¼ cup (either homemade or commercial)
Italian bread crumbs

Instructions

PREHEAT oven to 350°F.

DISSOLVE yeast into ½ cup tepid water. In large mixing bowl combine sugar, salt, and butter. Add 1 cup of boiling water and mix. Add to this mixture evaporated milk, eggs, yeast and mix. Add cheese, garlic, 3 cups of flour and mix. Mix 1 cup of remaining flour at a time until dough is stiff. Knead mixture on well-floured surface for about 2 minutes.

LET RISE for approximately 1 hour. Knead dough again on well-floured surface and shape dough into two loaves. Sprinkle crushed Italian bread crumbs on well-greased cookie sheet. Place loaves on cookie sheet and let rise for approximately 1 hour. Bake 25 minutes at 350°F.

Yields 2 loaves

A guest cabin at Jackson Hot Springs.

JACKSON OMELET

Recipe by Julia Richmond

Ingredients per serving

- 2 large eggs
- 1 tablespoon heavy cream
- 2 tablespoons butter
- 1 tablespoon diced onion
- 2-3 large mushrooms, diced (we use wild, but any kind is great)
- 1 tablespoon red, yellow, or orange bell pepper, diced
- 4-5 snow pea pods

- ¼ cup broccoli
- 1 tablespoon diced tomato
- ¼ cup fresh spinach
- 2 tablespoons ham, cooked
- 2 tablespoons sliced bacon, cooked crispy
- 2 tablespoons ground sausage, cooked
- 1 cup freshly grated sharp Cheddar cheese

Instructions

PREHEAT oven to 375°F.

COMBINE heavy cream and eggs; mix well. In a sauté pan combine onions, mushrooms, bell peppers, snow peas, and broccoli and sauté with 1 tablespoon of butter. Preheat a second sauté pan in the oven for 2 minutes. Coat preheated sauté pan with the remaining tablespoon of butter. When the butter has melted, add egg mixture; let cook for 15-30 seconds. Layer the vegetable mix over egg mixture. Add tomatoes and spinach. Add meat mixture over vegetables. Top with ¾ cup freshly grated Cheddar cheese.

BAKE in oven for 10 minutes in sauté pan. Check omelet at about 8 minutes. The consistency of the omelet should be solid. If you "jiggle" the pan all the egg mixture should be a solid texture holding together egg, vegetables, meat, and cheese.

To serve

FOLD omelet in half and remove pan from oven, sprinkle omelet with remaining ¼ cup of freshly grated cheese. Serve with whole-wheat toast, home fries (our version of hash browns), and fresh fruit.

Serves 1

SALMON AND SPINACH IN PUFF PASTRY WITH DIJON CREAM SAUCE

Recipe by Boni Roberts

So popular over the holidays that we had special requests for dinner parties.

For the Salmon

8 squares of puff pastry, 5 x 6 inches	½ teaspoon crushed red chile pepper flakes
2 cups fresh spinach leaves	¼ teaspoon garlic
8 tablespoons cream cheese	4 6-8 ounce pieces of salmon filet
Salt and pepper	

Salmon Cooking Instructions

PREHEAT oven to 350°F.

PLACE 4 or 5 leaves of spinach in middle of puff pastry square, place 2 tablespoons of cream cheese in center and sprinkle with salt and pepper. Then sprinkle with red chile pepper flakes and garlic. Place salmon filet on top of the cream cheese and spinach, sprinkle top of salmon filet with salt and pepper. Fold pastry up around sides of salmon. Place additional pastry square over entire stack, slightly stretch to tuck under. Brush with water along seam to seal. Bake in 350°F oven for 20 minutes.

Dijon Cream Sauce

½ cup white wine	2 tablespoon Dijon mustard
1 teaspoon of lemon juice	¼ teaspoon salt
¼ teaspoon fresh garlic, minced	Pinch of black pepper
1 ¼ cup extra heavy whipping cream	

Dijon Cream Sauce Cooking Instructions

IN SAUCEPAN over medium heat put in wine, lemon juice, and minced garlic. Bring to boil. Simmer to reduce by approximately half. Add cream, salt, pepper, and Dijon. Stir well. Simmer for 3 to 4 minutes until slightly thick. Serve sauce warm over Salmon Spinach Pastry.

Serves 4

BANANA NUT BREAD
Recipe by Delila Dawson

We use this bread as the base ingredient for our banana bread French toast and as our complimentary morning sweet pastry.

Ingredients

½   cup softened butter
1   teaspoon vanilla
3   large eggs (at lower altitudes, use one less egg)
¾   cup sugar
2   cups flour

1   teaspoon baking soda
½   teaspoon salt
½   cup sour cream
2   large, ripened, mashed bananas
1   cup chopped walnuts

Instructions

PREHEAT oven to 375°F.

CREAM butter, vanilla, eggs, and sugar. Add flour, baking soda, and salt. When the mixture is well blended, add sour cream, bananas, and walnuts. Mix well.

POUR into 9 x 5 x 3-inch loaf pan. Bake for 65 minutes at 375°F.

Yields 1 loaf

Triple Creek Ranch

Established 1982

5551 West Fork Road
Darby, Montana

Turn west from Hwy. 93 onto West Fork Road (Hwy. 473). Drive 7½ miles to Triple Creek Ranch sign

Open year-round

Dining Room open to public (depending on availability) Reservations 6:00 to 8:30 pm Please call ahead 406-821-4600 Fax: 406-821-4666 tcr@bitterroot.net www.triplecreekranch.com

Main lodge.

Triple Creek Ranch

Barbara and Craig Barrett, Owners
Judy and Wayne Kilpatrick, General Managers
Jason Willenbrock, Chef
Ana Willenbrock, Pastry Chef

Triple Creek Ranch, an internationally renowned Relais & Chateaux property, is an exceptional destination resort for discerning travelers who desire a small world-class facility near Montana's spectacular outdoor activities. Located in the Bitterroot Mountain Range of the Montana Rockies, Triple Creek Ranch is situated on 450 acres of wooded hillside bordered by national forest in three directions.

The original owner purchased the land that is now Triple Creek Ranch in 1982 and built what he believed to be the ideal mountain retreat. Many-time guests, Barbara and Craig Barrett of Arizona purchased Triple Creek Ranch in September 1993. General managers Judy and Wayne Kilpatrick have been full-time residents on the ranch since its beginning.

Triple Creek Ranch boasts 19 beautifully appointed cabins nestled under towering Ponderosa pines. All cabins have wood-burning fireplaces, direct dial phones with separate dataports, voice mail, satellite television, VCR, and a fully stocked bar. Some cabins feature a separate living room and bedroom, steam shower, and hot tub on the deck. Freshly baked cookies are delivered daily to cabins.

Guests enjoy a variety of exhilarating year-round outdoor adventures. In winter they ride horseback through fresh powder, snowshoe along a ridgeline, or snowmobile the high country. Excellent skiing, both cross-country and downhill, is just 30 minutes away. For relaxation, options include experiencing a private in-cabin massage, enjoying the soothing hot tub in the pine-scented forest, or curling up with a good book beside a crackling fire. An on-ranch fitness center is available for those who wish to stay in shape. Popular summer activities include hiking, tennis, fly fishing, whitewater rafting, swimming, horseback rides, cattle

Main lodge dining room.

Triple Creek Ranch, Darby

108

drives, and ATV rides. Golfers practice on the ranch putting green and then play golf in nearby Hamilton. Some guests choose to take in the majestic mountain views on a Hummer ride. History buffs learn Native American culture or trace the trail of Lewis and Clark on a guided tour. With binoculars in hand, wildlife enthusiasts spy on elk, white-tailed and mule deer, moose, and wild turkeys that live on the ranch. A few even experience the thrill of sighting mountain lion cubs, bald eagles, and on a rare day, an elusive golden eagle.

At the center of Triple Creek Ranch sits an impressive log-and-cedar lodge straddling a picturesque creek. Edged by enormous picture windows and tiers of balcony decks, the soaring structure shelters a rooftop lounge, a library, and an intimate dining room, and serves as the focal point for social activity.

In the evening, guests sample hors d'oeuvres and fine wine while visiting in the lounge. World-class cuisine is savored in the candlelit dining room with entrées such as Herb Crusted Rack of Lamb coated with rosemary, Dijon mustard and Panko, served with black truffle potato purée and merlot-thyme jus. A stroll under the dazzling starlit big sky of Montana ends the perfect day at Triple Creek Ranch.

Jason and Ana Willenbrock.

Fine dining in an elegant setting.

CARAMELIZED FENNEL AND POTATO SOUP

Makes 2 quarts

Ingredients

1 ounce clarified butter	½ cup sherry
2-3 fennel bulbs, julienne	½ cup Pernod
¼ onion, minced	2 quarts chicken stock or broth
1 tablespoon shallot, minced	Salt and white pepper to taste
½ tablespoon garlic, minced	Heavy cream to taste
¾ tablespoons dry thyme	Sliced black truffle
3 potatoes, peeled and diced	Sliced chives
½ cup white wine	

Preparation

IN stockpot heat butter to smoking point. Add fennel and caramelize well. Add onion and sauté. Add shallots and garlic and sauté. Add thyme and potatoes and cook for a couple of minutes, stirring; deglaze with wine, sherry, and Pernod and reduce by half. Add stock and cook until potatoes are tender. Purée with beurre (handheld) mixer. Add cream to lighten color and season to taste.

GARNISH each bowl with two truffle slices and chives.

Herb and Mustard Crusted Rack of Lamb
(recipe follows).

HERB AND MUSTARD CRUSTED RACK OF LAMB

Ingredients

4	lamb racks, frenched, fat cap left on		1	tablespoon thyme, minced
½	cup Panko bread crumbs		2	tablespoons Dijon mustard
1	tablespoon rosemary, minced			

Preparation

MIX Panko and herbs together. Brush loin with mustard and roll in Panko. Roast in oven at 375°F for 20 minutes or until desired temperature.

Merlot-Thyme Jus

1	ounce clarified butter		1	bunch thyme
3	tablespoons minced shallots		2	cups demi-glace
½	bottle merlot		1	cup softened butter
4	sprigs rosemary			

Preparation

SWEAT shallots in butter. Deglaze with merlot and reduce by half. Steep herbs; turn off heat and let sit for 30 minutes. Bring to quick boil, stirring, and add demi-glace. Thicken if necessary with slurry (thin paste of water and cornstarch). Monte au beurre (swirl in softened butter).

Serves 4

TRUFFLE POTATO PURÉE

Ingredients

6	Idaho potatoes, peeled and diced		3	finely-diced black truffles
2	ounces whole butter		¼	cup truffle oil
½	cup heavy cream, heated			Salt and pepper

Preparation

STEAM potatoes until tender. Put in mixer with paddle; add butter, cream, and salt and pepper. Mix until creamy. Adjust if necessary. Fold in truffles and oil. Serve with the Rack of Lamb.

Serves 4

POLENTA CRUSTED SALMON MEDALLIONS

Ingredients

4	7-ounce salmon filets cut in half width-wise
½	cup polenta paste seasoned with thyme, ginger, salt and white pepper
	Chervil/Dill Sauce
	Morel mushrooms, quartered

Ramps (or leeks) julienne

Asparagus blanched, extreme bias julienne

Carrots, julienne finely and blanche

Julienne beet chips (Finely julienne beets and fry in 300°F oil until crisp)

Chervil/Dill Sauce

½	ounce clarified butter
1	tablespoon shallot, minced
1	teaspoon garlic, minced
1	cup white wine
2	cups heavy cream

2	bay leaves
2	tablespoons chervil, minced
2	tablespoons dill, minced
	Salt and pepper to taste

Preparation

SAUTÉ shallot in butter until translucent. Add garlic and sauté 30 seconds. Deglaze with wine and reduce demi sec (by half). Add cream and bay leaves and reduce until nappe consistency (coats a spoon). Add herbs and adjust seasoning. Hold in water bath.

IN SMOKING hot skillet, sear salmon medallions on flesh side until nice dore (golden brown). Remove and cool. Coat each salmon medallion with polenta paste and sear polenta side down until polenta crisps and browns. Flip medallions, being careful not to destroy crust, and lightly sear other side. Finish in oven.

IN SAME PAN, sauté ramps (or leeks), asparagus, and carrots. Finish with light sauté of mushrooms and cover with sauce.

PLACE Salmon Medallions one on top of the other and spoon Chervil/Dill Sauce ragout around plate. Garnish with julienne beet chips.

Serves 4

TUNA MARTINI
with Wasabi Mayonnaise and Sesame Tuile

Ingredients

1	Soku block tuna or sushi grade Ahi tuna divided into 4 portions (approximately 2 ounces each)
¼	large red onion, finely minced
½	tablespoon sesame oil
2	teaspoons rice vinegar
2	scallions cut extreme bias julienne

1	tablespoon Wasabi Tobikko Caviar
	Salt and white pepper to taste
1	cup cooked sushi rice
4	Sesame Tuile (recipe follows)
4	teaspoons Wasabi Mayonnaise (recipe follows)

Preparation

FINELY mince tuna on impeccably clean cutting board. Toss with red onion, oil, vinegar, and salt and pepper.

PLACE one to two tablespoons of cooked rice into bottom of martini glass. Top with tartare mixture. Top mixture with dollop of mayonnaise and sprinkle with scallions and Tobikko. Place tuile standing upright in center of tartare.

For the Wasabi Mayonnaise

1	cup mayonnaise	2	tablespoons soy sauce
1½	tablespoons Wasabi powder		

MIX all ingredients together and let sit 1 hour. Adjust amounts of soy and wasabi to taste.

For the Sesame Tuiles

2	egg whites	1	ounce melted butter
	Pinch of salt		Sesame seeds to taste
½	cup sugar		Sesame oil to taste
¼	cup all-purpose flour		Honey to taste

Preparation

MIX ingredients well and let sit 1 hour. Spread on a Silpat® (nonstick baking pan liner ideal for baking cookies and patisseries) or coat a heavy baking sheet well with cooking spray or line with parchment paper. Bake at 350°F for 4-5 minutes.

Serves 4

SEASONAL FRUITS IN A TROPICAL BROTH

Ingredients

Fresh seasonal fruits   Muscat Sabayon
Tropical Broth   Almond Tuile

For the Tropical Broth

3   cups water   3   limes, zest and juices of
2   cups sugar   3   bananas, sliced

BRING the water and sugar to a boil; pour over the lime juice, zest, and bananas. Let cool. Strain.

For the Muscat Sabayon

2¾   ounces sugar   8½   ounces heavy cream
¾   cup Muscat   4   egg yolks

REDUCE the sugar and Muscat to the consistency of syrup; whisk in the cream and yolks. Continue whisking over a water bath until thick, so that the egg yolks cook as they thicken into a light, foamy custard.

For the Almond Tuiles

⅓   cup all-purpose flour   ½   orange, zest of
¾   cup confectioners' sugar   2   egg whites
½   lemon, zest of   3   tablespoons melted butter

WHISK all ingredients. Spread on a Silpat® (or parchment liner) on a heavy baking sheet. Sprinkle the sliced almonds over the top and bake at 350°F for 4 minutes. Tuiles may be made 2 days in advance and kept in an airtight container at room temperature.

To Serve

ASSEMBLE fresh seasonal fruits on serving plates, top with Tropical Broth. Spoon the Muscat Sabayon on the Almond Tuile. Gratinée (brown) Sabayon with a blow torch and place on top of the Fruit Soup.

Serves 4

The
Bridge
Neighborhood
Bistro

515 South Higgins
Missoula, Montana
Reservations: 406-542-0638
Delivery: 406-542-0002
www.bridgebistro.com
Open 7 days a week

Dinner at 5:00 pm
Delivery and Drive-thru opens
at 11 am (600 South Higgins)

Closing time is generally around
10 pm, but varies seasonally

The Bridge

David McEwen and Shirley Juhl, Owners & Chefs

For the last three decades in the same location, David McEwen and Shirley Juhl have owned and operated one of Missoula's most long-lived restaurants. The Bridge is a true Missoula "find." This small and casual restaurant has been popular with the locals for many years.

Shirley, who owns The Bridge along with husband David, started a restaurant at this same location in 1971 called The Gilded Lily. They originally opened the restaurant to feature French and Indonesian fare. Now, the restaurant is more of a "neighborhood bistro" serving a varied and changing menu. The historic "Butterfly Building" of Missoula was built in 1908 on the south side of the Clark Fork River. It originally housed a grocery store at street level with a "Dime-a-Dance Hall" above.

Shirley is a third generation Montana gal who was raised in Helena in an extended family that operated a restaurant there for many years. While it has not always been easy, she has always exhibited the old Montana tenacity and continues to operate an independent and successful establishment and is a first-class chef.

Today the restaurant occupies the front part of the street level or you can walk up the original wooden stairs into a small intimate setting and look out over the Clark Fork River. There is also a theatre and banquet hall in the back.

The Bridge features wild game along with their extensive wine list—22 offerings by the glass and 10 local microbrews on tap.

The Bridge's comfortable dining rooms.

The Higgins Street Bridge over the Clark Fork River. The Bridge Restaurant is in the tall building at the extreme right of the photo.

TILAPIA
WITH PECAN BUTTER

A rich New Orleans/Cajun style dish. Tilapia is an African freshwater fish. You may substitute another fish if you like. Snapper or catfish will work. The secret to this dish is the court bullion. We make ours from shrimp and lobster shells along with pieces of trimmed fish.

For the Pecan Butter

¼ pound soft butter

1-2 limes, juice of

½ cup pecans

For the Fish

2 cups court bullion (seafood stock)

2 teaspoons minced garlic

¼ cup roux

¼ cup Worcestershire sauce

1 egg

½ cup milk

3 pounds fresh tilapia

¼ cup Cajun blackening spice

1 cup flour

Oil for pan frying

Salt

Preparation

MAKE the butter in a food processor with the "S" blade. It should have a very distinct taste of lime. Blend all ingredients until nuts are fine and mixture is creamy. Set aside.

BRING the stock with the garlic to a boil and add the roux to thicken. Add Worcestershire and season to taste.

BEAT egg and milk together. Coat fish with Cajun spice. Dredge fish fillets in egg mixture, then flour. Fry in a hot oiled pan until golden and done.

SERVE the fish on a bed of the Meuniere sauce. Top with a generous dollop of the pecan butter.

Serves 6–8

NOTE: *A standard court bullion is made by setting a fish-pot on the stove with a mixture of white wine and vegetable broth (along with shrimp and/or lobster shells), seasoned with sliced onion, parsley, a carrot, a rib of celery, a chunk of unsalted butter, and salt and pepper to taste. Simmer the court bullion for about a half hour, and then cook your fish in it. This court bullion will work with any sort of fish.*

Linguine with Roasted Garlic, Red Peppers & Pine Nuts

A simple and flavorful dish that has been very popular at The Bridge. We call it "Dave's Linguine" on our menu.

For the Pasta

1	cup peeled garlic cloves	2	pounds linguine
2	tablespoons olive oil	2	red bell peppers
1	cup pine nuts	½	cup parsley
2	cups vinaigrette (recipe below)		Salt and pepper

For the Vinaigrette

½	cup lemon juice	1	cup olive oil
2	tablespoons Dijon mustard	2	teaspoons salt
1	tablespoon dried basil	1	teaspoon pepper

Preparation

PREHEAT oven to 350°F.

WHISK together vinaigrette ingredients in order given, add olive oil slowly, set aside.

ROAST garlic in olive oil on pan in 350°F oven for 30 minutes, cool and chop fine. Roast pine nuts for 10 minutes, set aside.

GRILL peppers on open flame (stovetop or grill) until skins are black. Peel off the skins under cold running water and slice peppers into thin strips. Canned roasted peppers may be substituted. Cook and drain linguine.

TOSS all vinaigrette and pasta together in a large bowl and season to taste.

Serves 10-12

Red Bird Restaurant

120 West Front Street
Missoula, Montana
Hours, 5:30 to 9:30 pm

406-549-2906
Reservations recommended
Call for directions

The Red Bird extends a warm welcome.

Red Bird

Jim Tracey, Owner & Chef

The original Florence Hotel, built on this site in 1888, offered weary railway travelers and settlers a comfortable night's lodging. The hotel was formerly known as "America's Finest Small Hotel." When it burned in 1913, the Florence was rebuilt as a major 160-room hostelry and was a longtime regional gathering place until it, too, was destroyed by fire in 1936.

Missoula's lack of a major hotel had serious implications, and even though the nation was then in the midst of the Depression, Walter H. McLeod and other influential businessmen secured community support to rebuild. When the elegant new Florence Hotel opened in 1941, Spokane architect G. A. Pehrson masterfully designed the $600,000 "jewel of a hotel" in the new Art Moderne style. Characterized by its rounded corners and horizontal emphasis, terra cotta and glass blocks accent the shiny-smooth concrete and metal surfaces. The splendid 140-room hotel boasted the Northwest's first central air conditioning system, novel glass shower doors and first-class interior appointments in a "harmony of color." One of only two local examples of the style, the third generation Florence reflects the town's steadfast regional importance into the 20th century, the growth of tourism, and the civic pride that prompted its construction.

The Red Bird, a restaurant with new ideas in a historic location, brings back the finest of dining to this historic landmark.

Opened in 1996, Christine Littig turned the restaurant over to her chef Jim Tracey in 2002. The Red Bird continues to change with the times and the seasons. With a passionate staff, Red Bird creates "Edible Artwork" time and time again.

In 2001 Missoula was rated first in Montana and fifteenth in the nation for preserving historic resources. In 1999, it was also named "the Great American Place" by *American Heritage Magazine*.

The early Florence Hotel before it burned.

The third Florence Hotel today.

ASPARAGUS SOUP
with Lemon

Ingredients

2	tablespoons butter	1 ½	pounds asparagus, woody bottoms removed
1 ½	yellow onions, sliced or chopped	1 ¼	cups heavy cream
3	celery stalks, chopped	1	teaspoon sugar
3	Yukon Gold potatoes, peeled and chopped	2	lemons, freshly squeezed juice
½	cup white wine		Kosher salt and cracked pepper to taste
7	cups chicken stock or broth	6	cups water
¼	cup fresh Italian parsley, chopped		

Preparation

COOK onions and celery in butter over medium to medium-high heat until tender or translucent. Add the potatoes and cook for another 2 minutes, stirring constantly. Add white wine (this is called deglazing), then chicken stock and parsley. Simmer (bring to a slight boil where one area is bubbling) for half an hour.

MEANWHILE, bring 6 cups of water to a boil and add asparagus to this until asparagus is tender but still bright green and not overcooked. Remove asparagus from water and add to soup. Blend soup in batches until smooth (be careful with hot soup when blending). Add cream, sugar, salt, pepper, and lemon to soup base and heat over low heat. Taste and adjust seasoning to your preference. This soup can be garnished with poached asparagus tips, lemon wedges, unsweetened whipped cream, or cracked pepper.

Serves 4-6

SPINACH SALAD
with Orange Ginger Cream Dressing

For the Salad

2 ½   *cups freshly-picked spinach, stemmed*

For the Dressing

4   *oranges, juiced*
1   *tablespoon minced ginger*
¼   *cup cream*

2   *tablespoons olive oil*
2   *tablespoons rice wine vinegar*
   Salt and pepper to taste

Preparation

REDUCE the orange juice and the ginger in a small pot to about a third of its original volume. Strain to remove the ginger and then blend with the remaining ingredients. Taste. This should make enough dressing for about six salads depending on the size.

TOSS spinach with the salad dressing with tongs or by hand, then top with anything you like. For instance; a grilled half an orange, sliced red pepper, cashews, and sesame seeds all go well, in addition to grilled and marinated duck breast. Sure to be a pleaser.

Serves 4

GRILLED LAMB
with Mint and Currants

For the Lamb

1   frenched rack of lamb, cut into individual medallions on the bone (2 per person, use more if desired)

For the Potatoes

3   Yukon Gold potatoes, boiled and mashed (preferably through a ricer)

⅛   cup parsley, chopped

⅛   cup basil, chopped

2   tablespoons melted butter

⅓   cup cream, warmed

   Salt and pepper to taste

For the Currant Sauce

1   tablespoon olive oil

½   cup currants

¼   cup rum

½   teaspoon garlic, minced

¼   cup fresh mint

½   cup vegetable stock or broth

¼   cup dry white wine

¼   teaspoon cayenne

1   tablespoon honey

   Salt and pepper to taste

For the Tapenade

1   cup green olives, chopped

½   cup cherry peppers, chopped

1   red pepper, diced

¼   cup currants

¼   cup feta cheese

¼   cup parsley, chopped

COMBINE all of the potato ingredients in a pot and stir until combined and heat over low heat until hot (about 10 minutes). Combine all of the ingredients for the tapenade in a bowl. For the currant sauce, heat the olive oil in a pot; add the currants and garlic. Cook for 1 minute. Add the remaining ingredients and cook over medium-high heat for 15 minutes (don't cook away all of the liquid). Blend until smooth, and then reheat when ready to serve. Everything until now can be made ahead of time and reheated.

LAST, season the lamb on both sides with kosher salt and fresh cracked pepper then grill until medium rare (about 4 minutes on each side depending on the thickness, it may be less).

TO SERVE, spoon potatoes in a wide bowl or deep plate. Surround with sauce, using a spoon. Place lamb ribs on potatoes. Place tapenade wherever it looks good. This is great garnished with a spoon of plain yogurt with mint leaves sticking out. Don't forget to taste for salt and pepper the whole time you are preparing.

Serves 4

THE WILD MONTANA HUCKLEBERRY

Montana has an abundant supply of wild huckleberries, but commercial picking and severe drought are putting a dent in recent crops. Many animals such as grizzly and black bears are extremely dependent upon these tasty, succulent berries for survival.

While huckleberry domestication has potential, attempts to grow huckleberries commercially in fields during the past century have failed. It is difficult to duplicate the conditions that huckleberries need in the wild; the correct slope, aspect, shade, moisture, and climatic conditions that they need to survive. Research is underway to develop plants and cultural practices that will allow huckleberries to be grown domestically. Management and harvest of wild huckleberry stands may be viable commercial alternatives to natural production.

For people interested in huckleberry conservation or are unable to pick their own in sometimes steep, mountainous terrain—an alternative berry, the annual garden huckleberry (*Solanum melanocerasum, syn S. nigrum guineense*) is commercially available from a few sources. The plant produces an abundant crop of small dark purple fruit. One plant should produce enough berries for a single pie. The fruit does not taste like the wild huckleberry when picked, as it is not at all sweet, but a pleasing berry taste does come through surprisingly well when it is cooked with plenty of sugar. It can be used as a viable substitute for blueberries in pies, jams, jellies, sauces and candies. It is very hardy and easy to grow, even in cold climates at higher elevations, and that is perhaps the main thing that it has going for it.

Ask your local nursery or search the Internet to find more information and how to obtain the garden huckleberry.

Double Arrow Resort

Highway 83, Mile Marker 12
Seeley Lake, Montana

Hours, 5 pm to 9 pm daily

406-677-2777
or 1-800-468-0777
www.doublearrowresort.com

The Double Arrow Resort
Bryce Finn, Chef

In the late 1920s, Jan Boissevain and Colonel George F. Weisel purchased a stock ranch in western Montana known as the Corbett Ranch. Boissevain, an avid horseman, dreamed of turning this property into a dude ranch, which he would name after the brand on his favorite horse.

His dream became reality in 1929, when the Double Arrow Ranch was established as the first commercial dude ranch at Seeley Lake.

It took about a year to transform the Corbett Ranch into the Double Arrow "dude ranch." Three log "Scully" cabins were moved from the Trail Creek area and located at the Double Arrow building site. After a winter of hard work several of the present ranch buildings were finished.

During the construction period, Boissevain made a trip East to drum up some opening trade. On July 1, 1930, the president of Cornell University and his wife arrived with other notables as guests.

By 1932, the Great Depression had caught up with the recreation business and the Double Arrow was struggling to stay afloat. In the fall of that year, the Indians came over the Jocko Pass to camp and hunt on Double Arrow land. Boissevain felt that they had a right to use the land as they always had and he welcomed them. Being unaccustomed to his strange manner and his accent, the Indians didn't care for him at first, but later grew to like him. They never learned to pronounce his name but there was a big dinner bell that he rang and they nicknamed him "the Bell Boss." In summer they often put on their ceremonial costumes and danced for the guests.

During Depression days, Missoula County contracted with the Double Arrow to house about one hundred unemployed lumberjacks, setting up double bunks from a nearby logging camp in the guest cabins. The ranch kitchen, which had been equipped to serve royalty, now served these men who found themselves out of work.

The ranch also provided work for a number of local people throughout the Depression. Herb Townsend, a horse breaker remembered a particular lady who was "a mighty good hand in the kitchen." But the woman looked out the window one day just in time to see a mountain lion making his way across the yard. Now, this wasn't in her contract at all. They had to take her back to Missoula the next day, and the Double Arrow was in the market for a new cook.

By 1938 Boissevain had tried just about everything to ward off hard times. He even tried starting a ski resort on the hillside behind the ranch buildings.

The beginning of World War II in 1941 delivered the final blow to Jan Boissevain and the dude ranch at the Double Arrow. He offered his services to the United States Armed Forces but was not accepted because of his age and his failing eyesight. In 1942 he auctioned off the ranch and the business and moved to California.

In the 1940s and early 1950s, the Double Arrow Ranch saw several owners and operators. Among them were Ray Cory and Whitey Rahn, Hollywood filmmakers.

C. B. and Helen Rich purchased the Double Arrow in the fall of 1958 from Jack Lanham of Missoula. Rich had been an outfitter and packer in eastern Montana for many years and when Yellowstone Park managers killed off thousands of elk where C. B.'s main camp had been, he was forced to look elsewhere for a packing/outfitting headquarters.

In 1966, C. B. and Helen sold the ranch to John Parker and Harold Mildenberger from Hamilton. The Rich family kept the pack outfit and leased the ranch back from the new owners. "By that time, I believe every roof on the place was leaking, some of the foundations sadly needed repair, and it was easy to see that we had gotten behind in our maintenance and repair," C. B. said.

At this time, C. B. and Helen terminated their lease with the ranch, but kept their pack outfit. That same year, the ranch was sold to Herb Richards, president of Life of Montana. He immediately began restoring the buildings. Log buildings were sanded inside and out. The first well was drilled, since the water supply for the buildings had previously come from Drew Creek. The buildings were completely redone, including plumbing, wiring, and roofing. Oak ranch furniture from Texas was imported to decorate the lodge. It was during these years that the controversial subdivision of the ranch began.

In 1977, John Trippe put together a limited partnership and purchased the ranch. They finished restoration of the buildings and added a swimming pool, tennis court, some condominiums and a hot tub building.

In 1989 the lodge once again changed ownership. A group of six couples from the Seattle area, all with Montana roots, purchased the lodge.

Since then, the historic Double Arrow Lodge has undergone significant improvements, while keeping intact its highly valued charm and cozy ambiance. All original cabins have been remodeled and upgraded and new lodging units were added in the '90s. A challenging golf course opened in 1994.

Providing a quality dining experience has been a commitment of the current owners. Every dish is a culinary treat for the palate and eye, skillfully prepared from the freshest ingredients by an exceptional chef. This unique ranch still offers the color of Montana with a fascinating history and excellent cuisine.

—*Excerpts of the history taken from the book* Cabin Fever.

FOIE GRAS SALAD

Ingredients

3   2½-ounce portions of Grade A foie gras (duck or goose liver)

15   whole dried figs cut in half

6   tablespoons balsamic vinegar

2   tablespoons lavender honey

2   teaspoons toasted sesame seeds

¼   teaspoon light sesame oil

½   cup Grand Marnier (reserving one tablespoon for later)

1½   teaspoons extra virgin olive oil

16   ounces of quality mesclun mix (wild salad greens)

2   scallions, julienne on a bias (slant)

2   medium green apples

Preparation

PLACE the portions of foie gras that have been cleaned of any veins and cross-cut scored for appearance into Grand Marnier to marinate. Marinate for 30 minutes, remove from liqueur and pat dry.

IN a small saucepan, combine the sesame seeds, ⅛ teaspoon of sesame oil, 5 tablespoons of balsamic vinegar, and the lavender honey. Bring this mixture to a boil and reduce it down in your pan until it will nicely coat the back of a metal spoon. Add the dried figs and toss to coat, set this pan aside to cool.

SEAR the foie gras portions on all sides over medium heat until golden brown (about 1½ minutes per side). Remove the pan from the heat and immediately begin to assemble the wild greens portion of this dish.

TOSS the wild greens using a metal bowl with the 1½ teaspoon olive oil, the reserved Grand Marnier, the remaining ⅛ teaspoon of sesame oil, and the remaining balsamic vinegar. Toss the greens to lightly coat them for flavor, place the field greens in the center of the plate, being gentle so as to create height from the stacking of the leaves. Place the portions of seared foie gras on top of the greens and using a spoon, drizzle the vinegar honey reduction across the salad using quick motions to create broken lines of sauce. Arrange the warmed figs around the outside of the salad and garnish with green apple wedges and julienne scallions. Enjoy!

Foie Gras Salad.

DOUBLE ARROW SEAFOOD PAELLA

Ingredients

1	pound of littleneck clams	2	tablespoons garlic, chopped
1	pound of black mussels	⅛	cup sun dried tomatoes, julienne
2	pounds of peeled and de-veined jumbo prawns	½	cup of fresh Roma tomatoes, diced
½	pound of sliced andouille sausage	2	cups basmati rice
4	3-ounce lobster tails split in half	4	cups cold water
4	crab claws	2	tablespoons butter
2	portabella mushrooms, large dice	1	tablespoon olive oil
½	green onion, chopped	¼	teaspoon saffron
			Salt and pepper to taste

Preparation

IN A medium saucepan bring the 4 cups of water, basmati rice, saffron, and butter to a boil. Add salt and pepper to taste remembering that the fresh seafood will bring its own saltiness to the dish as well. Cover the pan and reduce the heat to low and cook until almost all of the water has been absorbed.

PREHEAT oven to 350°F.

IN A large oven-proof skillet that preferably has a lid, add the olive oil and chopped garlic. Cook the garlic over medium heat until it just begins to brown, add

Seafood Paella.

all of the remaining paella ingredients, reserving the Roma tomatoes for the end so as to allow them to retain as much firmness as possible. Cook all ingredients together in the skillet just until the shrimp begin to turn pink and curl. Add the already hot saffron rice to the skillet and stir all ingredients together. Place the skillet into a preheated 350°F oven and bake for 25 minutes, stirring frequently. When the clams and mussels begin to open the dish is done. Remove from oven and add the Roma tomatoes. Serve in the skillet or plate each portion individually. Serve with your favorite chilled white wine.

Serves 4

ZINFANDEL POACHED PEARS

Ingredients

2   cups white zinfandel wine
½   cup sugar
2   cinnamon sticks
4   Bosc pears
¼   cup lemon juice, freshly squeezed

½   cup sour cream
¼   cup Melba Sauce (purchased or homemade)
2   puff pastry sheets
    Strawberries (optional for garnish)
    Fresh mint

Preparation

PEEL and core the Bosc pears and rub them with freshly squeezed lemon juice so that they do not turn brown before they are poached. In a 2-quart saucepan add the white zinfandel wine, sugar, and cinnamon sticks. Add the peeled pears. Cover the saucepan with tinfoil and place it over a burner on medium heat. Cook the pears until they are fork tender; do not overcook. Remove the pears from the pan and discard the cinnamon sticks. Reduce the sweetened white zinfandel wine over medium heat until it gains the consistency of syrup.

THOROUGHLY chill the poached pears in a refrigerator. Cut the puff pastry sheet length-wise into ½-inch slices. Starting at the bottom of the pear using the puff pastry to plug the whole in the bottom from when it was cored begin to wrap the puff pastry strips around the pear. (You can use your finger dipped in water to help adhere the strips together.) Continue adding strips until you reach the top of the pear. Repeat this with all of the pears. Bake in a preheated 400°F oven until the pears have turned golden brown.

IN A bowl, combine the sour cream and the Melba Sauce together. Using a spoon or pastry bag, fill the hollowed out area of the cored pear with the sauce just before serving. Add a fresh mint sprig to the top, serve with your favorite vanilla ice cream and drizzle with the reduced wine syrup.

Melba Sauce was created by the famous French chef Auguste Escoffier for Australian opera singer Dame Nellie Melba. To prepare, force 1 cup canned or fresh raspberries through a sieve fine enough to hold back the seeds. Add ¼ cup sugar and cook 6 minutes, or long enough to make a heavy syrup (216°F).

Serves 4

*Zinfandel poached pears
at the Double Arrow.*

La Provence Restaurant

408 Bridge Street
Bigfork, Montana

Open year-round
Reservations recommended

Deli open, 11:00 am to 2:00 pm
Dining room, 5:30 to 9:00 pm
406-837-2923

La Provence in Bigfork.

La Provence

Caroline & Marc Guizol, Owners and Chefs

On July 1, 2000, La Provence Restaurant opened its doors to the public, dedicated to bringing a fresh and unique culinary experience to the Flathead Valley of Montana. Nestled in the quaint village of Bigfork, La Provence features French Mediterranean cuisine, prepared with care by Chef Marc Guizol, a native of the south of France and former Dining Room Chef at the Ritz Carlton of Naples, Florida, and Chef at Palace Court Restaurant at Caesars Palace in Las Vegas.

The menu at La Provence changes seasonally. The cuisine features many of the sun-drenched flavors typical of the south of France which have been blended with local products to create a unique fusion of French and Northwestern American flavors. In 2002, La Provence received *Wine Spectator* Magazine's Award of Excellence for their extensive international wine list.

La Provence features several small dining rooms, decorated with warm colors to create a comfortable and light atmosphere. In addition, a large atrium houses the Wine and Tapes Bar. In 2002 a banquet room, The Lavender Room, was built upstairs from the main restaurant and can seat up to 60 people for private parties and receptions. In the winter months La Provence can seat up to 130 customers in one seating, and in the summer the deck allows an additional 60 outdoor guests. For lunch there is La Petite Provence Deli, daily featuring delicious sandwiches served on French baguettes, homemade soups, fresh salads, and quiche. They have also established a catering service over this past year.

Marc and Caroline Guizol.

About the Owners

Chef Marc was born and raised in a small village in the south of France, right in the heart of Provence. Ever since he was young, he found himself in the kitchen, first helping his mother with the family meals and then in a local restaurant taking the first steps in his career in the food service industry. After working in Italy for a while, Marc returned to France to satisfy his national military duties, serving as personal chef to one of France's top generals. He later moved to England to work at the Four Seasons Inn at the Park Hotel as well as at several world-renowned restaurants in London. After serving as Executive Sous Chef and Acting Executive Chef at the Reids Palace Hotel in Madeira, Portugal, Chef Marc moved to the United States to serve as the Dining Room Chef of the Ritz Carlton Beach Resort in Naples, Florida, where he met his wife-

Chef Marc enjoying a creation from La Provence.

to-be. While at the Ritz, he received the Ivy Award, won a national competition sponsored by Baccardi and Johnson and Whales University and was responsible for the dining room being granted the Mobile Four Star rating and the coveted AAA Five Diamond Award.

From there, Marc took the position as chef at the Palace Court Restaurant at Caesar's Palace in Las Vegas, but soon moved on to Bigfork to turn his dream of owning his own restaurant into a reality.

Caroline grew up in Maryland. After receiving a bachelor's degree in Communications, she then moved on to Johnson and Whales University in Providence, Rhode Island where she graduated Suma Cum Laude with a bachelor's degree in Culinary Arts. After interning with two nationally recognized chefs in New Orleans (John Folse and Greg Sonniers) she worked in the banquet department of the Ritz Carlton in Naples, Florida and at Grey Oaks Country Club in an upscale golf community.

Marc and Caroline Guizol moved to the Flathead Valley early in 2000 with their twin boys, Zachary and Theodore, and their new addition, Nicholas. They currently live in Bigfork.

RACK OF LAMB
With Provençal Salsa Sauce

For the Lamb

2   tablespoons cooking oil

2   racks of lamb

Salt and pepper to taste

For the Provençal Salsa

1   cup diced tomatoes

2   tablespoons pesto

1   sprig fresh rosemary, chopped

¼   cup Kalamata olives, chopped

Preparation for the Salsa

COMBINE all the ingredients in a small mixing bowl and allow the flavors to steep at room temperature for at least 1 hour. Cover and refrigerate until ready to use.

For the Sauce

2   cups beef brown sauce, simmered
     to reduce to 1 cup

1½   cups red wine (a burgundy),
     simmered to reduce to ½ cup

Salt and pepper to taste

Optional herbs, such as Herbs de
Provençe or fresh rosemary

COMBINE the reduced brown sauce and reduced wine. Continue simmering to combine flavors and reduce slightly. Add salt and pepper and herbs to taste. (This is called a "traditional wine sauce.")

THEN mix one cup of the traditional wine sauce with 4 tablespoons of the prepared Provençal Salsa.

Preparation

PREHEAT oven to 375°F.

SEASON the lamb with salt and pepper. In a large skillet over medium-high heat, sear the racks on all sides. Remove the skillet from the stove and transfer to the oven. Cook for approximately 10 minutes or until desired internal temperature is achieved. Remove the racks from the oven and allow to rest on a cutting board in a warm place for 10 minutes. In a small saucepan heat the red wine sauce to a boil. Add the salsa and simmer for a few minutes. Adjust the seasoning with salt and pepper as desired and set aside.

WHEN ready to serve, portion the racks by slicing between the rib bones and arrange on serving plates. Spoon the sauce over the lamb and serve immediately. You can accompany this dish with seasonal vegetables and potato gratin.

La Provence, Bigfork

BUTTERNUT SQUASH SOUP
with Mussels

Ingredients

2 tablespoons olive oil	3 cups chicken stock
1 butternut squash, peeled, seeded, and cut into cubes	½ teaspoon Spanish saffron
½ medium-sized onion, peeled and chopped	1 cup heavy cream
1 teaspoon chopped garlic	Salt and pepper to taste

For the Mussels

1 cup white wine	1 dozen mussels, cleaned and de-bearded
1 cup water	
2 sprigs of fresh thyme	

Preparation for the Mussels

IN A large stockpot bring to a boil the white wine, water, and thyme sprigs.

ADD the mussels; cover and steam the mussels just until they open. Remove the mussels from the pot and reserve the cooking liquid to add to the soup later. Once cool, remove the mussels from the shells, setting them aside, then discard the shells.

For the Soup

IN A large stockpot, heat the olive oil over medium-high heat. Add the squash and onions and sauté for 3 to 4 minutes without allowing the onions to take on any color. Add the garlic, the chicken stock, and the cooking liquid from the mussels. Bring to a boil then reduce the heat to low and simmer for 15 minutes or until the squash is tender. Remove from the heat and purée with a hand mixer or in batches using a blender. Return to the stockpot and add the cream. Re-warm and add the mussels. Season to taste with the saffron, salt, and pepper. Serve immediately.

LAVENDER HONEY
CRÈME BRÛLÉE

Ingredients

5	egg yolks		1	tablespoon lavender honey
1	whole egg		1	tablespoon dried lavender
2	cup heavy cream		3	tablespoons sugar
2	tablespoons sugar			

To make the Brûlée

PREHEAT oven to 275°F.

IN A large bowl, combine all ingredients with a wire whisk until well blended. Pour mixture evenly into custard cups. To cook the custards evenly, you need to prepare a bain-marie: Place the custard cups in a 2-inch deep baking dish, transfer to the oven and very carefully pour warm water into the baking dish so that the cups are sitting in a warm bath of water. Cook until the custard is just set without browning the top, approximately 20 minutes. Remove from the oven and cool in the refrigerator.

WHEN ready to serve, remove from the refrigerator. Sprinkle the sugar evenly over the top of the custards. If you have a torch, brown the sugar evenly across the top, being careful not to scorch it. If you do not have a torch, place the custards under a hot broiler, watching carefully, allowing them to brown as evenly as possible. Serve immediately.

Lavender and Honey Crème Brûlée.

Painted Horse Grille

110 Main Street
Kalispell, Montana
Hotel Reservations 1-800-858-7422
Dinner served Monday-Saturday

Lunch served Monday-Friday
406-257-7035 or 406-755-8100
grand@kalispellgrand.com
www.kalispellgrand.com

The Painted Horse Grille in the Kalispell Grand

C. M. & Janet Clark, Owners
Brett Morris, Chef

Charbroiled Buffalo Striploin.

The Kalispell Grand Hotel offers historic accommodations and fine dining for the discerning traveler in the Painted Horse Grille, all just 30 minutes from Glacier National Park in Montana's magnificent Flathead Valley.

From the inception of the frontier hotel business, this hotel was known for its finer amenities. In 1912, the Kalispell Hotel hosted the relatively well-to-do traveller at a charge of $2 per night. This was considered twice the going rate of other hotels at that time. However, being situated in the heart of Kalispell's downtown business district and offering such privileged services as running water, door locks, and wake-ups, the Kalispell Hotel rarely hung out its vacancy sign.

The three-story brick structure, designed by Kalispell architect Marion Riffo and built by local contractor B. Brice Gilliland, has stood through the years as a silent sentinel to the changes in the Flathead Valley and downtown Kalispell. During World War I, information about the war was shouted to crowds of people at the corner of First and Main. In 1919, the City of Kalispell installed a water fountain on the corner where the hotel still stands, emphasizing the importance of the First and Main intersection. On weekend nights, the Opera House crowd would gather around the fountain and frequent the hotel lobby. Several patrons would eventually stay the night.

Famed western artist Charlie Russell was a good friend of Frank Bird Linderman, a noted writer who leased and managed the hotel from 1924 to 1926. Linderman, Russell, and author Irvin S. Cobb were close friends and on occasion took lunch together and then would saunter back to the hotel lobby's stuffed leather chairs. Here they would sit and exchange thoughts and stories of the West. Linderman, who lived the life of a true plainsman, migrated up the Missouri, and continued overland to settle in Kalispell. He later wrote books and novels that are still eagerly sought after by book collectors across the country. Charlie Russell's work is world-renowned, and found only in the finest art galleries today.

Through the years, a number of individuals have owned the hotel. At one point in the 1930s, the owners planned extensive renovations, including the addition of a fourth floor and what would have been Kalispell's first passenger elevator. These renovations never occurred; however, between 1939 and 1941 the interior of the Kalispell Hotel was remodeled. According to a contemporary newspaper description:

" . . . The modern hotel room of today has to be definitely different than that of some few years ago, as most of the travelling public of today carry radios and electric razors in its luggage, and demands box springs and inner spring mattresses for sleeping comfort. An entirely new plan of interior decoration has been carried out that is highly attractive to the eyes and gives the guest who steps within its hospitable doors and immediate feeling of physical well being and luxury as well as appealing to his aesthetic sense."

After early prosperity, the hotel fell on hard times during more recent decades and was reduced to taking in weekly, monthly, and even hourly tenants.

But in 1989, a major renovation began that brought the hotel back to vibrant life. The 51 "bath down the hall" rooms that had rented for $120 to $150 per month were transformed into 40 rooms with private baths, furnished in Victorian-style cherry wood.

The hotel reopened to guests in 1991 while renovation of the lobby continued. Today, the sweep of the original lobby can be seen, including the original oak stairway and the high, pressed-tin ceiling.

Early in Kalispell's history, there were eight downtown hotels, and today, only one remains—the Kalispell Grand Hotel. Inside the gracious lobby, guests can still envision the life and history of a bygone era. The Kalispell Grand Hotel is a living landmark in downtown Kalispell.

The hotel's restaurant, The Painted Horse Grille, offers some of the finest dining in the Flathead Valley. In its casual, upscale atmosphere, Chef Brett Morris prepares his creative dinner cuisine, including pasta entrées, succulent steaks, roasted pine nut encrusted salmon, rosemary-lingonberry rack of lamb, and Indian curry spiced duck breast. For lunch experience a variety of fresh salads, homemade soups, paella, and an array of homemade baguette sandwiches. Creatively prepared lunch and dinner specials are offered every day. Exquisite desserts, an extensive and well-selected wine list, and a full liquor selection complement your dining experience.

The Kalispell Grand in the 1920s.

The Kalispell Grand today.

MIXED STEAMED SHELLFISH

The Mixed Steamed Shellfish appetizer is a clam bake in a bowl, a unique blend of flavors that makes for a delicious combination. This recipe comes from the childhood memories of Chef Brett Morris.

Ingredients

6	fresh steamer clams		1	tablespoon chopped fresh basil
6	fresh steamer mussels		2	tablespoons chopped onion
6	¼-inch thick slices of Italian link sausage (pre-cooked)		1	teaspoon chopped fresh garlic
4	tablespoons butter		¼	cup Pernod (French liqueur)
¼	cup dry sherry		4	lemon wedges
1	cup clam juice or fish stock		1	tablespoon diced pimento
				Chopped fresh parsley

Preparation

HEAT butter in a large skillet (12-inch diameter). Add onion, garlic, basil, pimento, and a pinch of salt and pepper. Add shellfish and sausage; sauté, tossing every 10 seconds for 1 to 2 minutes. Add sherry and Pernod and reduce briefly. Add clam juice, bring to a boil, cover and cook until shellfish opens wide (2 to 3 minutes).

POUR mixture into two large individual bowls, garnish with lemon wedges and chopped parsley.

SERVE with a crusty bread to enjoy the sauce.

Serves 1–2

PAINTED HORSE GRILLE FISH STOCK

1	large onion, sliced		2	teaspoons white peppercorns
1	each celery stalk, sliced		1	bay leaf
2	pounds fish bones		1	sprig fresh thyme
1	cup dry white wine		2	sprigs parsley
1	teaspoon salt		2	quarts water

WASH the fish bones in cold water twice before making the stock. In a large pot, combine all ingredients, bring to a boil and simmer for an hour. Strain through a fine strainer.

Makes 2 quarts

CHARBROILED BUFFALO STRIPLOIN
with Brandy Morel Mushroom Cream Sauce

The Buffalo Striploin complemented with a Brandy Morel Cream Sauce is one of our most popular special entrées. Our guests sing praises of the tenderness and taste.

For the Meat

Prepare a hot grill

4 8-ounce buffalo strip steaks lightly seasoned with salt and pepper

For the Brandy Morel Mushroom Cream Sauce

3-4 tablespoons butter

¼ cup chopped onion

2 teaspoons chopped garlic

½-1 cup chopped or sliced fresh morel mushrooms (dried morels re-hydrated in warm water and drained and sliced may be used)

½ cup brandy

1 cup demi-glace or rich brown stock

1 cup heavy cream

Salt and pepper to taste

Roux, if needed (a mixture of flour and fat used as a thickening agent)

Preparation

PREPARE sauce first and keep warm while broiling steaks.

PLACE buffalo over hot coals or gas grill and broil until desired temperature (medium rare is suggested).

SAUTÉ onion, garlic, and mushrooms in butter in a saucepan or large skillet until browned. Remove from heat and add brandy. Place back on burner and flame, burning off the alcohol. When flame subsides add demi-glace or stock, bring to a boil and reduce one-half to one-third volume.

ADD heavy cream and reduce by boiling till desired thickness is reached. Add salt and pepper to taste. If you are preparing sauce ahead of time, whisk in a little roux to keep sauce from breaking up.

Serves 4

Roasted Curried Duck Breast
with Apricot-Pistachio Demi-Glace

This is the signature dish of The Painted Horse Grille—a dish to die for with flavors of curry and apricots, served over basmati rice. Chicken breast can be substituted for the duck.

Meat Ingredients

4 6-8 ounce boneless duck breasts—*skin on, rolled with ground cumin, salt and pepper, and Madras curry powder*

To Prepare Duck

PREHEAT oven to 400°F.

HEAT olive oil in sauté pan, add prepared duck breasts (meat side down). Sear for 1 to 2 minutes. Turn breasts over and roast in the pan, skin side down for 15-20 minutes.

Apricot Pistachio Demi-Glace Ingredients

2 *leeks (white part only), trimmed, washed, and chopped*
2 *tablespoons olive oil*
1 *sprig fresh rosemary*
2 *tablespoons crushed juniper berries*
1 *teaspoon Madras curry powder*
1 *teaspoon ground cumin*
½ *cup sliced dried apricots*
2 *tablespoons honey*

½ *cup roasted shelled pistachio nuts*
2 *tablespoons balsamic vinegar*
2 *tablespoons white wine vinegar*
½ *cup dry gin*
2 *cups demi-glace or rich brown stock*
1 *teaspoon chopped garlic*
   Mixed cornstarch and water to thicken sauce

To Prepare Apricot Pistachio Demi-Glace

HEAT olive oil in a 4-quart saucepan, sauté leeks and garlic for 30 seconds to 1 minute. Add rosemary, juniper berries, curry powder, cumin, balsamic and white wine vinegar, ½ tablespoon of the apricots, and honey. Whisk together to make a paste. Remove pan from heat, add the gin, whisk into paste. Place pan back on heat and flame the mixture to burn off the alcohol. (Be careful when lighting the mixture.) After the flame has gone out add the demi-glace or stock and reduce by boiling or simmering to half the volume. Strain through a fine sieve into another stockpot.

ADD pistachio nuts and remaining apricots. Bring to a boil and thicken as desired with the cornstarch and water mixture.

To Serve

SLICE duck breasts crossgrain. Place breasts on individual plates or serving plates. Spoon Apricot Pistachio Demi-Glace sauce over and serve over basmati rice.

Serves 4

LEMON MASCARPONE CHEESECAKE
with Black Raspberry Sauce

Crust Ingredients

1 cup graham cracker crumbs	⅓ cup melted butter
¼ cup sugar	Zest of 1 lemon

To Prepare Crust

PREHEAT oven to 350°F.

MIX graham cracker crumbs, sugar, and lemon zest together, add melted butter, mix until moist. Press in bottom of ungreased 9-inch springform pan. Bake for 10 minutes at 350°F.

COOL on rack while cheesecake batter is being prepared. Wrap springform pan bottom with foil before baking in water bath.

Cheesecake Ingredients

3 8-ounce packages cream cheese, softened	1 fresh lemon, including zest (4 tablespoons juice)
1 cup mascarpone cheese	4 tablespoons flour
1 cup sugar	1 tablespoon vanilla
2 eggs	

To Prepare Cheesecake Filling

PREHEAT oven to 350°F.

BLEND cream cheese with electric mixer until soft, add sugar, mascarpone, zest of 1 lemon, lemon juice, and vanilla. Mix until all ingredients are well-combined and smooth. Add eggs one at a time on low speed just until mixed in (about ½ minute). Stir in flour by hand. Do not overmix.

POUR the batter into prebaked graham cracker crust (with foil-wrapped bottom). Bake in preheated oven in water bath (shallow pan with about 1 to 2 inches of water) for 1 hour. Turn oven off and let stand for 30 minutes with oven door closed.

Black Raspberry Sauce

COMBINE 1 quart fresh or frozen black raspberries with 1 cup of sugar in a stainless steel bowl and leave at room temperature. Pass thawed ingredients through a food mill until seeds are removed, leaving a thick, smooth sauce.

To Serve

CUT in cheesecake wedges and spoon black raspberry sauce over.

Visit the Flathead Valley in late July for luscious
orchards full of sweet dark cherries.

Cafe Max

121 Main Street
Kalispell, Montana
406-755-7687

Open for Dinner
Tuesday-Saturday 5:30 pm
Reservations recommended

Cafe Max

Douglas and Vonnie Day, Owners
Douglas Day, Chef

Chef and owner Douglas Day.

Cafe Max is located in historic downtown Kalispell. Chef Doug Day earned his culinary degree from Johnson and Wales University in Providence, Rhode Island, and worked in some of the country's most notable restaurants in Florida, the Virgin Islands, and Seattle before opening Cafe Max in 1996. The restaurant is renowned for exquisite food and professional service. Chef Day was voted "Best Chef in the Flathead Valley" and Cafe Max "The Flathead Valley's Best Fine Dining Restaurant."

The menus at Cafe Max change frequently to follow the elements of the seasons, emphasizing ingredients from the Pacific Northwest. Seafood dishes are prepared with king salmon, halibut, and ocean scallops from the cold, clear waters of Alaska.

Menus include premium Angus beef, lamb, veal, chicken, and vegan entrées, as well as an extensive selection of wines and fabulous desserts. In keeping with the philosophy of the dinner menus, the wine list is an eclectic selection from around the world with an emphasis on the wines of Washington and Oregon. Cafe Max frequently hosts popular six-course wine dinners and more casual evenings of food and winetasting, which include discussions of each wine and the food with which it is paired.

Chef Doug Day invites anyone with questions about Cafe Max recipes to email him: *chezday@centurytel.net.*

GALLATIN VALLEY GOAT CHEESE FRITTERS
with Wild Greens

For the Fritters

1	12-ounce log of Gallatin Valley Goat Cheese (or other soft white goat cheese)
½	cup flour
2	eggs
½	teaspoon salt

1   tablespoon water
1   cup Japanese bread crumbs (Panko)
    Olive oil for frying
    Fresh lemon juice
    Crushed pepper

For the Salad

Mixed wild greens
Extra virgin olive oil

Fresh-squeezed lemon juice
Cracked pepper

Preparation

DIP a sharp knife in hot water and slice goat cheese into 8 rounds, about ¾-inch thick. Lightly roll each one in flour.

IN A small bowl, beat eggs with salt and water. Dip each flour-coated round of cheese into the egg mixture, then roll in Panko and set aside. Heat oil to 375°F in a deep frying pan (oil should be about 3 inches deep). Fry Panko-coated cheese rounds, 2 or 3 pieces at a time, until golden brown, approximately 2 minutes on each side. Drain on paper towels.

SERVE immediately over wild greens drizzled with extra virgin olive oil and fresh lemon juice. Sprinkle with cracked pepper.

BREAST OF DUCK WITH FLATHEAD CHERRY SAUCE

Ingredients

4 boned duck breast halves

3 tablespoons butter

2½ tablespoons sugar

2 Macintosh apples, peeled, cored, and chopped

2 cups syrah or cabernet sauvignon

2 pounds (about 4 cups) fresh Flathead cherries, pitted (can use any sweet cherries)

⅛ teaspoon cinnamon

4 whole cloves

¼ teaspoon nutmeg

   Salt and pepper

1 cup water

Preparation

MELT sugar in 2 tablespoons butter in a large skillet over medium heat. Turn heat to medium-high, add apples and cook, stirring frequently until softened and browned, about 8 minutes. Add red wine and reduce for 4 minutes.

LOWER heat to medium, add 1 cup water, 3 cups cherries, cinnamon, cloves, and nutmeg. Season with salt and pepper. Mash cherries with a wooden spoon, then simmer mixture until liquid is reduced by half, 15-20 minutes.

STRAIN sauce through a fine sieve, then return to skillet. Add remaining cherries and simmer over medium heat until sauce has reduced by a third, about 8 minutes. Reduce heat to low.

SCORE the fat side of the duck breasts and season both sides with salt and pepper.   Heat a large skillet over medium heat. Add duck breasts with the fat side down and cook until the skin is crisp, about 12 minutes. Pour off excess fat. Turn and continue cooking for 6 to 8 minutes more.

REMOVE duck from skillet and slice thin. Whisk remaining 1 tablespoon butter into sauce and spoon over duck.

APPLEWOOD SMOKED TENDERLOIN OF BUFFALO
with Horseradish Caper Cream

Ingredients

3	5-ounce medallions of buffalo tenderloin	1	tablespoon butter
	Salt and pepper		Vine-ripened tomato slices

SEASON medallions with salt and pepper, then sear in butter until browned on both sides, about 5 minutes. Place in heated smoker with applewood chips for 10 minutes, remove and chill.

Horseradish Caper Cream

2	tablespoons horseradish	1	tablespoon wild capers
2	tablespoons whipped cream		Salt
1	teaspoon lemon juice		

MIX first four ingredients together and add salt to taste.

SERVE Smoked Buffalo Tenderloins with sliced vine-ripened tomatoes and Horseradish Caper Cream.

Pollo Grill

Rotisserie & Bar

POLLO GRILL
ROTISSERIE & WINE BAR

Established 1998

Open 7 days, serving dinner
5:00 to 10:00 pm nightly
1705 Wisconsin Avenue
Whitefish, Montana

406-863-9400
pollogr@bigsky.net
Reservations@pollogrill.com
www.pologrill.com

Pollo Grill

Walter and Susan Nickerson, Owners
Walter Nickerson, Chef

Walter and Susan Nickerson opened the Pollo Grill on April 1, 1998. Since that time the restaurant has enjoyed much critical acclaim and wide popularity with locals and visitors alike. The menus and wine lists are ever changing to keep abreast of seasonal and market availability. Recently the Pollo won the *Wine Spectator* Award of Excellence. The atmosphere at the Pollo Grill is comfortable and casual and the attentive service ensures a wonderful experience. The well-trained staff offers insight to all questions of preparation and is quick to offer wine-paring suggestions.

Off-premises catering is another facet to the Pollo Grill. Walter has developed a fine reputation for producing, preparing, and serving dinner parties, cocktail parties, weddings, and reunions. The Pollo Grill can supply everything from planning, rentals of all equipment, setup and breakdown, and of course, all food, beverage, and service staff.

Summer brings many special items to the Flathead Valley, so the Pollo Grill shares the local bounty by featuring fresh fruits, vegetables, and meats throughout the season. They have a wide variety of specials for the season, including Montana grown elk, trout, and a delectable rack of lamb.

Statewide, Montana is home to some of the world's greatest trophy-trout streams and lakes. This allows the Pollo Grill to feature local delicacies such as Rainbow Trout in a Tri-colored Tortilla Crust with Cilantro Lime Sauce.

The legendary cherry orchards around Flathead Lake bloom in the spring and then produce lush, succulent white or bing cherries in early to mid-July. Walter teams these cherries with a specially seasoned Grilled Boneless Duck Breast, thinly sliced and generously sauced with these truly delicious native Montana cherries.

Both peppermint and wintergreen mint are grown here and used primarily for their very rich and strong oils. Some of this mint flavors a Mint Sauce which complements the Grilled Rack of Lamb.

Whitefish is regarded nationwide as an authentic recreation hot spot with boundless year-round activities and attractions because of its close proximity to Glacier National Park.

STEAMED LITTLENECK CLAMS WITH CHORIZO, FENNEL, GARLIC, AND WHITE WINE

We recently have uncovered a great supply of littleneck clams available to us on a very regular basis. This recipe is an adaptation to a well-known Portuguese preparation and uses the Mexican chorizo in place of the chourice. The texture of the chorizo gives the resulting broth more body and just screams to be sopped up with some great crusty bread. It is a simple, quick, and delicious appetizer.

Ingredients

2   pounds littleneck clams (Manila or mahogany clams can be substituted)

8   ounces chorizo

½   fennel bulb, julienne

2   garlic cloves, finely diced

2   cups white wine (the crispness of Pinot Gris or Sauvignon Blanc works best)

2   tablespoons of olive oil

Instructions

HEAT the olive oil in a 4-quart saucepan.

ADD the chorizo and sauté, stirring often until some color occurs (4 minutes). Add garlic and fennel; sauté another 2 minutes. Add clams and wine. Cover and cook until all clams have opened. Discard any that don't open. Serve in shallow bowls with plenty of crusty bread.

OUR suggestions for accompanying wines would be the Duck Pond Pinot Gris or the Omak Sauvignon Blanc.

Serves 4

Osso Bucco

with Gorgonzola and Rosemary Risotto

At the Pollo Grill we have chosen "comfort food" as our focus. Although the Rotisserie is a real focal point in our kitchen, one can always find daily features that revolve around the hearty, simple and more often classic methods of cooking. This recipe for Osso Bucco fits all of these categories.

Ingredients for the Osso Bucco

4   2-inch thick veal foreshanks
1   cup flour
2   cloves of garlic, finely diced
1   28-ounce can of crushed tomatoes

2   cups white wine (the other half of the bottle from the steamed clam recipe)
Salt and pepper

Gremulata

Zest of one lemon
½   bunch of parsley, chopped finely

2   cloves of garlic, finely diced

Risotto

2   cups arborio rice
5   cups chicken stock or broth
1   cup crumbled Gorgonzola cheese

2   tablespoons finely chopped fresh rosemary
2   tablespoons of olive oil

Cooking Instructions for the Osso Bucco

PREHEAT oven to 350°F.

DREDGE the veal foreshanks in the flour and brown in olive oil in a braising pan. When you have seared all surfaces and see a light browning, add the garlic and continue to brown for an additional minute or two. Add the crushed tomatoes and white wine, season with salt and pepper. Cover and place the pan in a preheated 350°F oven. After 1 hour, turn the oven down to 250°F and continue to cook for a total of 3 hours. You can hold your Osso Bucco in a warm 200°F oven for some time. It will want to fall off the bone.

Cooking Instructions for the Risotto

RISOTTO does take some attention, 15–20 minutes.

HEAT the chicken stock in a saucepan. In another pan, heat the olive oil and add the arborio rice, stirring so as to coat the rice thoroughly with the oil. Start adding the hot chicken stock 2 or 3 ounces at a time. Let the stock be absorbed and continue adding the stock slowly until rice has become soft. You want to add the stock slowly so a cream-like liquid develops. When the rice is soft, add the Gorgonzola cheese and rosemary, stirring to blend completely.

Cooking Instructions for the Gremulata

THIS is the simple part. Just mix together the lemon zest, parsley, and garlic. Although this could be looked at as just a garnish, rarely will you find anything that sets off the flavors in any dish as this does for Osso Bucco.

Presentation

ON a large dinner plate, we like to serve the Risotto in the center of the plate with the veal shank off to the side slightly. Generously spoon on the braising sauce from the skillet in which the Osso Bucco was cooked and top with the Gremulata. For the purist, we would also serve with a marrow scoop.

WINE suggestions are wide open; any full-bodied Cabernet pairs wonderfully with this hearty dish and always any Borolo or Chianti Antinori Chianti Classico, Aldo Morenco Barbera Pirona, Carmenet Dynamite Cabernet Sauvignon.

Serves 4

MIXED FIELD GREENS WITH RICOTTA INSALATA AND WHITE WINE VINAIGRETTE

Most produce sections in grocery stores today have a great selection of pre-washed and picked green mixes. You can use any mix you choose to complete this salad. I am using ricotta insalata cheese for its dryness against the tartness of the White Wine Vinaigrette. You could use feta or almost any wet goat cheese, Gorgonzola, or other bleu-veined cheese and be very happy with the results.

Ingredients

1	8-ounce package of mixed field greens
4	ounces ricotta insalata or your choice of cheese
2	ounces white wine vinegar
8	ounces olive oil blend
1	teaspoon sugar
⅓	red onion, finely diced
	Salt and pepper to taste

Preparation

WASH greens and pat dry. Put them in a large salad bowl with the cheese crumbles and diced red onions. In a separate bowl mix the oil and vinegar, sugar, salt, and pepper. Dress and toss to your liking just before serving.

Serves 4

Produce departments now display great selections of pre-washed greens.

Cannoli with Shaved Chocolate

If you were inclined to serve this entire menu we think something on the light side would be a wonderful finale. Our Cannolis are just that, and to top that off even further we suggest a half bottle of Nivole Muscat d'asti.

Ingredients

8 prepared cannoli shells*	1 teaspoon vanilla extract
2 pound ricotta cheese	1 teaspoon almond extract
2 cups confectioners' sugar	1 block semi-sweet chocolate

Instructions

PLACE the ricotta in a fine mesh sieve and drain completely. Add the sugar and extracts and whip with a fine piano wire whip until smooth. Pipe the Ricotta mixture into the shells using a pastry bag and a medium star tip.

GRATE the chocolate directly over the cannolis so that they become sprinkled generously. Serve two to a person.

*Prepared cannoli shells can be purchased at specialty food stores or ordered off the Internet (see Culinary Sources, page 207).

Tupelo Grille & Wine Bar

Established in 1995

17 Central Avenue
Whitefish, Montana
406-862-6136

Dinner served daily at 5:30 pm
(Reservations accepted only for
parties of six or more)

Patrick Carloss.

Tupelo Grille & Wine Bar

Missy & Patrick Carloss, Owners
Patrick Carloss, Chef

Southern cooking in Montana? No matter what the temperature is outside, Tupelo Grille on Central Avenue is always one of Whitefish's hottest dining spots. The Tupelo Grille was established in 1995 by Patrick and Missy Carloss, and it has quickly become one of Montana's favorites for locals and tourists alike. Specializing in Cajun Creole cuisine, Louisianan chef and owner Patrick Carloss provides a unique dining experience with a taste of the bayou.

Along with Carloss's terrific menu came a new sophistication in décor. Southern folk art and photography line the textured walls. Local diners, along with skiers from nearby Big Mountain, cluster in wooden booths and sneak peeks into the kitchen. Recently, the restaurant's wine list received a *Wine Spectator* Award.

While you're in Whitefish, look into the abundance of outdoor activities in the area—only 30 minutes from the West Glacier entrance to Glacier National Park, 30 minutes to Flathead Lake, and 10 minutes from Big Mountain Ski Resort. Whitefish's 1910 train depot still accommodates passengers daily as Amtrak passes through, making it an ideal train trip from the Northwest's major cities.

A Tupelo Grille Filet dish.

FENNEL-RUBBED PORK
TENDERLOIN
with Orange Glaze and Roasted Yams

For the Pork

2	pounds pork tenderloin (silver skins removed)	2	tablespoons sugar
4	tablespoons paprika	2	tablespoons salt
2	tablespoons ground fennel	2	tablespoons garlic powder
		1	tablespoon white pepper

PREHEAT OVEN to 375°F.

COMBINE ALL seasonings in shallow bowl. Place tenderloin into seasonings and rub until heavily coated. Heat heavy large nonstick skillet over high heat. Add pork and sear until brown all over, turning occasionally (about 5 minutes). Roast pork in oven until thermometer registers 160°F (about 30 minutes).

For the Yams

3	large yams or sweet potatoes (washed, peeled, and chopped in half-inch cubes)	½	tablespoons allspice
1	tablespoon fresh ground ginger	2	tablespoons olive oil
1	tablespoon brown sugar	1	tablespoon fresh thyme

PREHEAT oven to 350°F.

COMBINE all ingredients in mixing bowl and transfer to baking dish. Roast in oven for approximately 30 minutes or until yams are tender.

For the Orange Glaze

2	cups veal stock or canned beef broth	1	teaspoon balsamic vinegar
4	tablespoons orange marmalade		

COMBINE veal stock and marmalade in saucepan and heat until reduced by half. Add balsamic vinegar.

SLICE pork and fan over roasted yams, and ladle sauce over the top.

Serves 4

Tupelo Grille, Whitefish

161

CREAMY SHIITAKE AND PORTABELLA BISQUE

For the Bisque

1	large portabella mushroom, stems removed, sliced thinly
2	cups shiitake mushrooms, stems removed, sliced thin
2	cups button mushrooms
1	large onion
1	tablespoon minced garlic
5	tablespoons butter
2	tablespoons sweet sherry
1 ½	cups chicken broth or stock
3	cups heavy whipping cream
3	cups water
½	tablespoon fresh thyme
½	teaspoon salt
¼	teaspoon white pepper
3	tablespoons flour

IN PROCESSOR, finely chop onion and button mushrooms and transfer to medium saucepan on high heat with garlic and 2 tablespoons of butter. Sauté until onions have clarified. Deglaze pan with sherry. Add remaining ingredients, except for flour and remainder of butter, bring to a simmer. In separate saucepan, melt 3 tablespoons of butter and combine with flour, slowly whisking it into bisque. Serve with chopped chives.

Serves 4

Low country shrimp-and-grits, a Tupelo Grille favorite.

Tupelo Grille, Whitefish

Whitefish Lake Golf Club

Highway 93 near
Whitefish, Montana
406-862-5285 Fax: 406-862-5290
Lunch 11:00 am to 3:00 pm
Dinner 5:30 to 9:30 pm

(10:00 pm weekends)
Reservations recommended
E-mail: wlgcrest@aboutmontana.net
www.golfwhitefish.com

The Restaurant at the Whitefish Lake Golf Club

Owners Doug Reed and Dan Crumbaker
Dan Crumbaker, Chef

I In the 1930s, Whitefish Lake Golf Club, originally planned as a golf-baseball-airport complex, was built with much thanks to FDR's "New Deal" and the Works Progress Administration.

Local fundraising, contributions, and enthusiasm helped raise the $1,600 needed to purchase the 104-acre tract. The WPA funded the labor and locals built the original nine-hole course and airstrip.

Construction of the clubhouse or "administration building for a nine-hole airport" began in 1936. Using timbers from the surrounding forest, the lodgepole pines were crafted to create the crisscrossed beams overhead along with the walls and ceiling. The original clubhouse extended only to the far side of the bar and was completed in 1937.

On August 3, 1939 the first airplane landed at the course, causing considerable speculation for golfer safety. Planes continued to use the course into the early 1940s, even during golf tournaments, but golf soon took priority. The course was still designated as an emergency landing field into the 1950s and '60s.

A second nine holes was added in 1962 to create the woods/lake eighteen on the North Course. The South Course was built in the early 1980s and '90s.

The Whitefish Lake Golf Association com-

Driving from #8 Tee, Whitefish Lake Golf Course, Whitefish, Mont.

pleted a clubhouse renovation in 1999 that not only added necessary amenities, but also enhanced the beauty of the original structure. *Golf Digest* selected the courses as one of the top five for the state of Montana.

Today, owner/operator Douglas Reed and chef/partner Daniel Crumbaker operate the restaurant and uphold its reputation as one of the Flathead Valley's best in a rustic atmosphere serving elegantly prepared steaks, fresh seafood, and house specialties. With over twenty years combined working experience at the club they will accommodate your every need, from dining to catering or a special party. We trust you will enjoy your visit to this historic Montana setting.

Owners Doug Reed and Dan Crumbaker.

Coconut Shrimp with Pineapple-Mango Chutney.

Mixed Grill Rack of Lamb, Beef Tenderloin & Rabbit Sausage with Dried Cherry Sauce

Chef Daniel Crumbaker

Ingredients

2	pounds domestic lamb rack		4	shallots, chopped
12	ounces rabbit sausage		½	cup carrot, finely diced
2	pounds. beef tenderloin sliced into 4-ounce medallions		1	teaspoon garlic, minced
	Olive oil			Thyme and tarragon stems
1	pint pinot noir		1	bay leaf
1	pint rich veal stock (or use Knorr Swiss Demi-Glace in packets)		2	ounces whole butter
				Salt and whole black pepper
½	cup dried tart cherries, bloomed overnight in 1 cup pinot noir (retain this wine for use later)		1	teaspoon tarragon, finely chopped
			1	teaspoon parsley, finely chopped
			2	ounces whole butter, softened

For the Dried Cherry Sauce

BROWN any meat scraps from the tenderloin on all sides in 2 ounces whole butter. Add the shallot and carrot, brown lightly, discard the butter, and add the wine (including the wine from the soaking cherries) reduce it by three-quarters over high heat. Add the herb stems, whole black pepper, bay leaf, and garlic. Gradually add the pint of veal stock, in thirds, reducing each time until the sauce lightly coats a spoon. This should yield a generous cup of sauce. Pass through a fine sieve, add the soaked cherries, season, and reserve for serving. Mix chopped tarragon and parsley with softened whole butter. When the sauce is ready to be served, bring to a simmer and whisk in this herb-butter mixture until smooth.

For the Meats

IN LARGE sauté pan heat the olive oil over high heat and quickly sear the lamb rack on sides, remove and season with salt/pepper and the chopped herbs. Place whole lamb rack into 375°F oven for 30 to 35 minutes, depending on preferred doneness.

SHAPE the rabbit sausage into 1½-ounce patties and wrap in caul fat (the membrane from the lining of the abdomen of pork, or substitute bacon), season with salt and pepper. Also season the beef with salt and pepper. Midway through the cooking of the lamb, add the rabbit sausage and continue cooking until both are done. Remove from oven and let rack rest. Meanwhile quickly sear the steaks in the same pan the lamb and rabbit were just in. When the steaks are done, arrange one steak with one sausage onto warmed dinner plates. Finish with two chops carved off the rack and 2 ounces of the dried cherry sauce.

Serves 8

Coconut Shrimp with Pineapple-Mango Chutney

Chef Daniel Crumbaker

For the Chutney (*Yields about 3-4 cups*)

Prepare the Chutney at least two weeks before using. This enables the flavors to blend and mellow.

1	cup onion, diced	4	cloves
½	cup dried fruit, such as golden raisins	1	cup fruit vinegar, such as raspberry or cider vinegar
½	cup sugar		
2	cloves garlic, minced	¼	cup corn syrup
1	teaspoon. ginger, minced	½	cup water
¼	teaspoon. salt	1	pineapple—peeled, cored, seeded, and diced
¼	teaspoon. mustard seed		
½	stick cinnamon	1	mango—peeled, cored, seeded, and diced

MIX first 12 ingredients in a nonreactive (stainless steel) saucepan. Simmer over low to moderate heat for 15 minutes. Add fruit, and simmer until thickened. Cool and refrigerate until using.

Ingredients for the Shrimp

1	pound U-15 shrimp	2	cups Panko flaked bread crumbs
1	cup flour	8	whole eggs, whisked thoroughly
1	cup shredded coconut	8-10	cups oil for frying

Preparation

PEEL, de-vein, and butterfly. Mix shredded coconut with Panko bread crumbs. Coat each shrimp thoroughly in flour, then dip in egg mixture. Coat with bread crumb mixture, and set aside. Note: It helps to keep shrimp separated after breading. Heat oil to 350°F in heavy saucepan or fryer. Fry shrimp in batches, 3 to 4 at a time, until golden brown (approximately 3–4 minutes per batch). Drain on paper towels. Transfer to platter and keep warm. Serve with Pineapple-Mango Chutney.

Serves 6-8 as an appetizer, 4-6 as an entrée

Grinnell Glacier in Glacier National Park.

Snowgoose Grille

at

St. Mary Lodge

THE RESORT AT GLACIER
ST. MARY, MONTANA

Located at the East Gateway to Glacier National Park

Junction of Highway 89 and Going-to-the-Sun Rd., St. Mary, Montana

SUMMER ADDRESS
(April 16 - October 14)
The Resort at Glacier,
St. Mary Lodge
St. Mary, Montana
Dining 5:30 to 9:00 pm

FOR MORE INFO
Call or email
406-732-4431
1-800-368-3689
stmary@glcpark.com
www.glcpark.com

Snowgoose Grille at St. Mary Lodge in Glacier National Park

Roscoe Black, Owner
Bryan Motola, Chef

The Snowgoose Grille has a spectacular backdrop.

St. Mary Lodge got its start in the mid- to late twenties after the proprietors, Hugh and Margaret Black, met in Glacier. The year 1926 found Hugh Black working in Michigan and looking for a change of scenery. He heard that Chief Ranger Nick Carter was possibly hiring, so he and a friend fixed up a Ford Model T and drove across the country from Caro, Michigan. Hugh became a seasonal ranger fighting forest fires and helping with early park development.

When the road to Logan Pass was partially finished in 1930, Hugh became the first road patrolman in Glacier Park. This job included keeping traffic speed down and keeping bears out of the government road camps. He was furnished with a Ford pickup and a shotgun loaded with birdshot.

Margaret James grew up in St. Paul, Minnesota, and came to Glacier in 1928 as the executive secretary for the Park Company, which was then owned by the Great Northern Railroad. This beautiful lady met the dashing and handsome ranger and a budding romance ensued. Hugh and Margaret were married in 1932 and started St. Mary Lodge and Resort. He got a lease on the current St. Mary Lodge property with $1,000 and a month's paycheck, and started construction right away. He and his crew built one-room cabins as fast as they could. Visitors would ask if they had any more cabins available and they would answer, "No, but we'll have one by tonight." They would rent the cabins at noon while the carpenters were still working on them. They built more every year until they had over forty of these one-room cabins with wood stoves and water pails. These same cabins now house the seasonal employees. While work was being done on the cabins, Margaret played a major role in the operation of their first restaurant, The Curly Bear Cafe. She also did all the bookwork for the rapidly growing operation.

When World War II hit, gas shortages all but stopped visitor traffic in the Park. During this time, Hugh supplemented the resort's income by running cattle and cutting ice from frozen lakes for the Great Northern Railroad which ran from Williston, North Dakota to Spokane, Washington. This ice was used on hot summer days to keep products cool prior to the advent of the refrigerated car. Margaret was kept very busy with the running of St. Mary, but somehow, found time to raise six children, as well.

The Blacks continued their hard work at St. Mary and were rewarded in 1952 by the completion of St. Mary Lodge, which housed 27 new rooms, the gift shop, and the new St. Mary Cafe. The lodge was remodeled in 1975 when the lounge area was added to the front and an addition was put on the gift shop. In 1989, the restaurant was expanded and remodeled into what you see today. The name "Snowgoose Grille" was added at that time, coming from a restaurant that the Blacks ran the previous three years on Big Mountain in Whitefish.

The internationally famous Snowgoose Grille is rated one of Montana's top eating establishments and offers the best dining in the area. A remodel of the interior of the Snowgoose has just been completed, giving it a wonderfully comfortable atmosphere. Their reputation as one of the West's finest buffalo restaurants has garnered features in *The New York Times*, *Travel and Leisure Magazine*, *Northwest Travel Magazine*, and numerous other publications. They offer a wide variety of buffalo specialties, including prime rib, steaks, homemade sausage, appetizers, burgers, meatloaf, and unique specials throughout the summer. All meals are prepared with care and imagination using the freshest ingredients, herbs, and seasonings, combined with their own dash of Western flair. A basket of their famous hot sourdough scones and honey butter accompanies each dinner. Make sure to save room for a homemade dessert, because the Snowgoose's pastry chefs have been creating scrumptious huckleberry delights for decades along with a wide array of mouth-watering treats. They serve breakfast, lunch, and dinner from late May to October.

Although St. Mary Lodge "The Resort at Glacier" has seen many changes and improvements since 1932, one thing has remained constant: St. Mary Lodge is a family-run operation committed to providing guests a quality experience when visiting Glacier. The Black family, along with hundreds of past employees who are a part of St. Mary history, have succeeded in creating facilities that have earned St. Mary Lodge the reputation as *the place* to stay or visit when in Glacier.

Combining the breathtaking panoramic views of Glacier and their famous Montana hospitality, the Snowgoose Grille is a Glacier Park tradition and truly a must stop on any trip to Montana.

Buffalo Flank Steak

For the Marinade

1	pint beer (your favorite)	2⅔	tablespoons shallot, chopped
1⅓	cups Italian salad dressing	2⅔	tablespoons garlic, chopped
⅔	cup red wine	2⅔	tablespoons tomato paste
⅓	cup red wine vinegar	2⅔	tablespoons lime juice
½	cup soy sauce	1	teaspoon coriander
2⅔	tablespoons Worcestershire sauce	1	teaspoon white pepper
1⅓	tablespoons sesame oil	1	teaspoon salt

For the Buffalo

3 pounds buffalo flank steak

PREPARE a marinade of all ingredients and marinate steak a minimum of 6 hours, overnight is best.

BROIL steak over hot charcoal fire for 5 to 10 minutes on each side, depending on degree of rareness desired.

SLICE thinly across the grain and serve with Béarnaise sauce.

Serves 6

Béarnaise Sauce

For the Sauce

½	cup white wine vinegar*	½	teaspoon white pepper
3	each shallots, minced fine	2	sticks butter (1 cup)
2	tablespoons fresh tarragon, minced		

PUT vinegar, shallots, half the tarragon, and pepper in a small saucepan. Bring to a boil and reduce until liquid is nearly gone. Cook at an extremely low heat and whisk in cubes of cold butter until it is all incorporated. (Do not let this boil.) If too thick, then whisk in a little hot water. Stir in remaining tarragon.

*You may use ¼ cup of white wine and ¼ cup of white wine vinegar for a slightly different taste.

STRAWBERRY CHICKEN SALAD

For the Salad

6	grilled chicken breast halves, julienne	3	slices red onion rounds
		2	heads romaine lettuce, chopped
18	whole strawberries, sliced	1	batch Citrus Poppy Seed Dressing

TOSS romaine and strawberries with Citrus Poppy Seed Dressing. Divide equally among chilled salad plates. Top with a julienne chicken breast. Garnish with red onion rounds.

Serves 6

CITRUS POPPY SEED DRESSING

For the Dressing

½	cup sugar	⅓	cup lemon juice
1 ½	teaspoons salt	1	cup mayonnaise
1	teaspoon dry mustard	1 ½	tablespoons poppy seeds
1	tablespoon onion juice		

MIX sugar, salt, dry mustard, onion, and lemon juice and poppy seeds into the mayonnaise.

Serves (roughly) 8 salads

BEER CHEESE SOUP

Ingredients

1 ⅞ ounces butter

1 ⅛ ounces onion, minced

1 ⅞ ounces flour

1 ½ cups turkey stock

1 ½ cups milk, 2% lowfat

⅜ cup heavy cream

1 ⅞ ounces Cheddar cheese, grated

1 ⅞ ounces American cheese, grated

¾ cup beer

1 ⅛ dashes cayenne pepper

1 ⅛ dashes celery salt

Preparation

IN A 2-quart saucepan melt butter over medium heat. Add onions, cook till soft. Do not burn. Add flour to make roux, let cook for 7-8 minutes. Keep stirring. Heat milk, cream, and stock in separate pan until it reaches 160°F. Whisk milk mixture and stock into roux. Add cheeses and mix until well blended and mix thickens. Add beer and seasonings. Let simmer for 5 minutes. (Do not let boil.) Salt and pepper to taste.

Serves 6

Lake McDonald in Glacier National Park.

BUFFALO CROSTINI

Ingredients

1	each French baguette, 2-inch diameter, sliced ⅛-inch thick
½	cup olive oil
	Salt and pepper

12   ounces buffalo filet or rib steak, grilled rare
       Horseradish Sauce

Preparation

PREHEAT oven to 350°F.

SLICE baguettes and lay out on a cookie sheet (25-30 slices). Dab olive oil on each slice. Lightly salt and pepper. Bake in a 350°F oven till golden, about 10-12 minutes.

For the Buffalo

SALT and pepper steak and grill on both sides. Don't overcook. Chill or even lightly freeze steak. Using a sharp knife, shave off pieces of meat. Re-chill if it is too soft. Place a small rosette of buffalo shavings in the middle of the crostini and top with a drizzle of the Horseradish Sauce.

HORSERADISH SAUCE

For the Sauce

¼   cup sour cream
2   teaspoons prepared horseradish

Dash Worcestershire sauce

MIX all ingredients together and top the crostini bread slices with the prepared buffalo.

Huckleberry Mousse in
Chocolate Tulips

Ingredients for the Mousse

⅔ quart huckleberries (fresh or frozen)

⅝ cup sugar

1¾ teaspoons gelatin

⅝ teaspoon cinnamon

1¼ cups heavy cream, whipped

6 mint leaves

Huckleberries for garnish

Ingredients for the Chocolate Tulips

¾ pound bittersweet chocolate chips

1 small saucepan

1 stainless steel mixing bowl or a double boiler

1 sheet waxed paper

6 small balloons

Preparation for the Mousse

HEAT huckleberries, sugar, gelatin, and cinnamon in a saucepan over medium-high heat until berries are mushy. Run huckleberry mixture through sieve. Chill mixture until thick and syrupy. Fold gently into whipped cream. Pour into Chocolate Tulip cups. Garnish with extra berries and mint leaves.

For the Chocolate Tulip Cups

PLACE double boiler or saucepan with water over low heat, bring to a simmer. Place chocolate in the top of the boiler or mixing bowl and stir with a heat-resistant spatula until chocolate is about two-thirds melted. Remove from heat and stir until chocolate is completely melted. Cool down until it is about 90°F. Blow balloons up and tie. Grasping the balloons by the base, tilt and dip the balloon into the tempered chocolate to form "petals" with all sides joined at the base. Stand dipped balloons on a tray lined with waxed paper, chocolate side down. Repeat until all balloons are finished. Set aside in a cool place until tulips are set. Gently pierce balloons with a knife and remove from chocolate tulip.

FILL with the Huckleberry Mousse and garnish with mint leaves and reserved fresh huckleberries.

Ristorante Portofino

220 Central Avenue
Great Falls, Montana
406-453-7186
Reservations recommended

Monday-Friday
11:00 am to 9:00 pm
Saturday 4:00 to 9:00 pm
Closed Sundays

The Ristorante Portofino

Tina Germano and Massimo Viale, Owners
Mike Taylor, Chef

Ristorante Portofino opened in the Christmas season of 1999. The restaurant is co-owned by mother and son, Tina Germano and Massimo Viale. Both are natives of Portofino, Italy. Portofino is a small port town just outside of Genoa filled with all types of ships and people.

Ristorante Portofino brings the feeling and the flavors from this spot on the northwest coast of Italy to Great Falls, Montana. This restaurant prides itself on an extensive menu of genuine Italian foods prepared from scratch in their kitchen and offers wonderful wines and coffees made in authentic Italian style.

They are located in the heart of Great Falls, just steps away from the Civic Center, Paris-Gibson Square, and many interesting shops, art galleries, antique shops, and downtown hotels. It is their pleasure to bring a little of Italy into to your life while visitng Great Falls.

Make sure to visit the new Lewis and Clark Interpretive Center on the outskirts of Great Falls. Cultural exhibits and outdoor trails detail the 1804-1806 journey of the Lewis and Clark Expedition with focus on their interactions with the Plains Indians.

Black Eagle Falls near Great Falls as Lewis and Clark might have seen it.

SEAFOOD LINGUINI

Great dish for seafood lovers!

Ingredients

1 tablespoon extra virgin olive oil	8 shrimp
2 teaspoon garlic	8 medium-sized scallops
8 clams	2 ounces of calamari
1-1½ cups clam juice (depending on desired thickness)	1 cup of marinara sauce
	Salt and pepper
8 mussels	8 ounces of linguini noodles

Cooking Instructions

ADD in a medium-sized pan, the olive oil and 2 teaspoons of garlic. Sauté until golden brown. Then add the clams and mussels. Sauté for about 3-4 minutes. Then add the clam juice. Increase the heat and boil for about 2-3 minutes. Now add the remainder of the seafood and the marinara sauce. Season to taste. Cook until the clams open and the rest of the seafood are no longer raw.

IN A separate pan, boil the 8 ounces of pasta until firm to the bite. Drain the linguini and add to the seafood.

Serves 2

ASPARAGUS ROLLATINE

This makes a wonderful appetizer or can be served as a meal with an accompanying side dish.

Ingredients

2	fresh tomatoes (Roma or regular)	8	asparagus spears
½	cup onion, chopped	2	slices of provolone cheese
2	teaspoons basil	2	slices of prosciutto
2	teaspoons parsley		Flour
4	teaspoons chopped garlic	3-4	eggs
1-2	teaspoons olive oil		Bread crumbs
	Salt and pepper to taste		

Cooking Instructions

IN A medium-sized bowl, dice the tomatoes and half of the onion. Chop about 2 teaspoons of basil and parsley. Also chop about 4 teaspoons of garlic. Add 1-2 teaspoons of olive oil and salt and pepper to taste. Mix gently to combine and add basil, parsley, garlic, or pepper and salt as needed. Heat a medium-sized pan of water and blanch the asparagus spears. Wrap four of the spears with a slice of provolone and one slice of prosciutto. Then pass the wrap through flour, eggs, and finally, bread crumbs. Repeat for the other four spears. Then fry the wrapped asparagus and serve topped with the tomato mixture.

Serves 2

CHICKEN VALDOSTANA

This dish is a long-standing favorite on our dinner menu. A true Italian specialty, it is sure to make your mouth water.

Ingredients

1 whole boneless, skinless chicken breast	Bread crumbs
Thinly-sliced prosciutto	Flour
Mozzarella cheese	Garlic
Fresh spinach	Olive oil (extra virgin preferably)
3-4 eggs, beaten	Salt and pepper

Sauce

Brown gravy   Mushrooms

Marsala wine   Artichoke hearts

BEFORE cooking, pour the flour into one medium-sized bowl, and do likewise with the bread crumbs and eggs. Each should be in a separate bowl. Also mince or mash the garlic into a pan with about ⅓ cup of olive oil.

Cooking Instructions

SPLIT the chicken breast into two even halves. Remove any excess fat. Then slice the two halves horizontally into four pieces and pound out the four pieces.

For the Stuffing

SAUTÉ 8 ounces of spinach and garlic and olive oil; salt and pepper to taste. Then place 1 piece of prosciutto, a slice of mozzarella, and 4 ounces of the spinach between 2 halves of the chicken breast. Repeat this for the other halves of the breast. Then, to ensure that the stuffing stays in, pound the outer edges of the breast together. Take the stuffed breast and pass it through the flour, eggs, and then the bread crumbs. Then fry the chicken.

PREHEAT oven to 400°F.

IN A separate pan, add 1 cup of brown gravy, 2 ounces of Marsala wine. Toss in a handful of mushrooms and two artichoke hearts. Once the chicken is thoroughly fried, add it to the saucepan and place in the oven on high heat for approximately 15 minutes. Serve the chicken on a dish with veggie of choice or potatoes.

Serves 2

*You'll see this view from the footbridge across the Missouri River
close to the Grand Union Hotel.*

The

Union

Grille

Established in 1882

1 Grand Union Square
Fort Benton, Montana

Dining Wednesday through
Sunday 5:00 to 10:00 pm
Reservations recommended

Lodging available all week
(Breakfast provided for guests)

406-662-1882 or 1-888-838-1882

grandunion@3rivers.net
www.grandunionhotel.com

The Grand Union as it looks today.

The Grand Union – Montana's Oldest Operating Hotel

James & Cheryl Gagnon, Owners
Clayton Arakawa, Chef

The Grand Union Hotel gained a new lease on life following an award-winning restoration, supervised by the National Trust for Historic Preservation, the U.S. Parks Department, and the Montana State Historic Preservation Office, that preserved the historical character of Montana's oldest operating hotel and one of its most famous landmarks.

The hotel's history began in 1882, just 36 years after Fort Benton was founded and 7 years before Montana became a state. It was built at the height of Fort Benton's prosperity during the steamboat era on the Upper Missouri River.

With construction costs of $50,000, and with an additional $150,000 spent on furnishings, the newly christened Grand Union Hotel opened November 2, 1882 with the biggest party the city and territory had ever seen.

Within a year, however, the hotel's fortunes declined. The opening of the Northern Pacific Railroad to Helena in June and the Canadian Pacific Railroad to Calgary in 1883 dealt a mortal blow to Fort Benton and the Grand Union Hotel with the closing of the territory's most important highway, the Missouri River. Business in Fort Benton declined rapidly and in early 1884 the hotel failed and was sold at a sheriff's sale in May of that year.

Operating through Fort Benton's decline and the ascendance of newly established Great Falls nearby, the hotel continued to suffer and was sold to Mr. J. H. Green and Mr. B. F. O'Neal in 1899 for just $10,000. Messrs. Green and O'Neal undertook a major renovation of the hotel, installing steam heat, electricity, and men and women's toilets on every floor. Elaborate furnishings were sold or discarded and new fashionable oak and brass furnishings were installed together with a quarter-sawn oak faux paint finish over the varnished woodwork. Enamel found its way onto the upstairs woodwork at this time and the black walnut bar received a coat of white paint.

In 1917, with the world at war and the Homestead land boom on in Montana, local ranchers, Mr. and Mrs. Charles Lepley bought the Grand Union. In just two years, Prohibition closed the hotel's thriving saloon and dry weather, poor crops and falling prices brought on the Great Depression to Montana.

During the 1930s and '40s the Grand Union ran steadily downhill due to the dire economic conditions of the area. The bedrooms, once considered the "best in the West," gained a reputation for a permanent insect population and worn and broken furnishings.

Grand Union Hotel, Fort Benton

In the mid-1940s the Depression ended as agriculture rose to undisputed importance in Fort Benton and Chouteau County. In 1952, the hotel was sold again, this time to Mr. and Mrs. Harold Thomas. By then, the lobby, dining room, and saloon were ghosts of a once elegant era. Rooms were threadbare with straw mattresses still sprawling on sagging springs. Two public bathrooms on each of the three floors were the only personal sanitary facilities in the hotel. Upstairs, pieces of the once picturesque chimneys sometimes fell to the sidewalk due to weathering. Bats nested in cavities in the cornices. Soot from the chimneys sifted down the walls and birds flew in and out at will. The window frames were so loose in their masonry that a person could stick his hand through the cracks. Sun had warped the window moldings badly. Settlement of the building made the upper floors sag.

Mr. Thomas completed a one-man, multi-year restoration that is credited with saving the building. By the late '70s, Mr. and Mrs. Thomas were interested in retiring, but wanted to see the hotel pass into responsible hands interested in its preservation. Rejecting various offers interested only in salvaging the hotel's contents, antiques and brickworks, they agreed to sell the hotel in 1979 to a group of local farmers headed by Mr. and Mrs. Roger DeBruycker.

In 1983, the hotel was closed for renovation. Prior to completion, however, the project collapsed due to a failed financing plan and inadequate capitalization. In 1986, the hotel was sold at sheriff's sale to satisfy debts, and the building's contents were stripped and sold at public auction by the DeBruyckers. The building was then left abandoned pending sale until 1995 when native Montanans James and Cheryl Gagnon purchased it with a plan to restore and reopen the century-old hotel.

The Grand Union Hotel was elegantly restored to its original splendor, reopening on its 117th anniversary on November 2, 1999. Today, listed on the National Register of Historic Places, and recipient of various state and national restoration awards, the Grand Union Hotel is Montana's oldest operating hotel and proud to continue its tradition by once again providing one of the grandest lodging and dining experiences in Montana.

The Grand Union lobby.

An elegantly restored room.

VEGETABLE SOUP
Chef Clayton Arakawa

Ingredients

1	small onion, diced
3	cloves of garlic
1	carrot, peeled and diced
2	stalks of celery, diced
1	quart stock or broth
1	yellow squash, diced
1	zucchini squash, diced

1   cup cooked great northern beans
   (May add any of your favorite vegeta
   bles, such as can of diced tomatoes)

   Parsley, chopped
   Basil, chopped

Preparation

SWEAT onions, garlic, carrots, and celery for 5 minutes. Add chicken stock and bring to boil then reduce heat and simmer for five minutes. Add remaining vegetables and beans. Cook until vegetables are tender. Season with salt and pepper. Just before serving, stir in basil and parsley.

COCONUT SHRIMP
Chef Clayton Arakawa

Ingredients

12	large black tiger prawns
1	cup shredded coconut
1	cup plain bread crumbs

1   egg with 1 tablespoon water, mix well
¼   cup flour

Preparation

MIX coconut and bread crumbs well. Cut shrimp in half lengthwise. Dredge in flour. Dip shrimp into egg mixture. Cover shrimp with coconut mixture. Set aside.

DEEP fry in oil 350°F until golden brown. Serve Coconut Shrimp warm.

Serving suggestion

ALMOST any chutney will work as a dipping sauce—or try sweet Thai chile sauce, which is a great complement to the shrimp.

Serves 4

GRILLED PORK LOIN CHOP
Chef Clayton Arakawa

Ingredients

4	10-12 ounce center-cut pork loin with ribs attached
8	Granny Smith apples
½	cup golden raisins
1	cup apple cider
1	tablespoon cinnamon

1	teaspoon cardamom
¼	teaspoon cloves
¼	teaspoon nutmeg
	Salt and pepper
½	cup brandy (optional)

Preparation

SEASON the pork generously with salt and pepper. Over a low flame, grill chops until meat thermometer registers 155°F, or about 15-20 minutes. Peel and core apples, cutting into sixths. Combine all remaining ingredients in a medium-sized saucepan. Bring the apple mixture to boil and lower heat to a simmer. Stir occasionally, cooking apples till tender but not overcooked, or about 15-20 minutes.

Presentation

SERVE Grilled Pork Loin Chop over your favorite mashed potatoes with spiced apples.

Serves 4

The Grilled Pork Loin Chop.

The River Grille

1225 Custer Avenue
Helena, Montana
406-442-1075
www.rivergrille.com

Hours of Operation
Tuesday–Saturday
5 pm to 10 pm
Open year-round

The River Grille

Laura Fix and Ron Morris,
General Managers
Ron Morris, Chef

The River Grille is owned and operated by the Morris family of Helena, who has served restaurant patrons in the Helena area for over 75 years.

The River Grille opened in January of 1997 to great reviews. Co-owners Ron Morris and his wife Laura Fix operate the restaurant for the family. Laura, a baker by trade, runs the front-of-the-house operations and Ron, a Certified Executive Chef with the American Culinary Federation, runs the kitchen.

It is an upscale Euro Montana Bistro with casual dining in an elegant atmosphere. Great Montana steaks and prime rib are featured, with fresh seafood and unique specials being offered daily. The River Grille serves one of the largest Single Malt Scotch collections in Montana!

The River Grille is located in Helena—the City of Gold, the Queen City of the Rockies. The city was originally a mining camp that sprang up when gold, silver, and copper were discovered in the valley. Helena became the territorial capital and once had more millionaires than any other city in the United States.

Today Helena is the home of the Montana state capitol and a variety of businesses. Southwestern Montana's revitalized mining and metals processing industries are located here, and it is still rich in agricultural tradition.

River Grille, Helena

The Missouri River in the Gates of the Mountain Wilderness Area.

Relax in the beautiful lounge in the River Grille.

CREAM OF FOUR-ONION SOUP
This is the Signature Soup at the River Grille

Ingredients

1   stick butter (¼ pound)
1   pound onions, sliced ¼-inch thick)
1   clove garlic, minced
6   ounces leeks (white and green tender parts), sliced ¼-inch thick
2   ounces shallots, minced
½   ounce fresh ginger, minced
    Pinch of cayenne pepper
4   ounces flour

2   quarts chicken stock or broth
1¼ cups dry white wine
4¼ cups whipping cream
2   tablespoons brandy
1   tablespoon plus 1 teaspoon fresh lemon juice
1   tablespoon kosher salt
2   teaspoons white pepper
2   teaspoons sugar

Garnish

Durkee's Fried Onions
Fresh chives, minced

Procedure

HEAT butter in heavy-gauged soup pot over low heat. Add onions and sauté lightly for 10 minutes. Add sugar and simmer 10 minutes more. Add leeks, shallots, ginger, garlic, and cayenne. Cook 3-5 minutes, stirring frequently; add flour and let cook for 3-5 more minutes. Slowly mix in chicken stock and wine. Bring soup to a boil. Reduce to a simmer and add cream. Let soup reduce for 30 minutes. Add brandy, lemon juice, salt and pepper; let simmer for 15 minutes longer. Cool soup quickly in an ice-water bath and refrigerate overnight. Soup improves in flavor as it sits.

To Serve

HEAT soup in double boiler to 140-150°F. Garnish with fried onions and fresh chives.

Serves 8

TAGLIATELLE BOLOGNESE, LASAGNA STYLE

Meat Sauce Ingredients

1	pound lean ground beef, ½-inch pieces		2	tablespoons fresh garlic, minced
1	pound hot Italian sausage, ½-inch pieces		3	large red peppers, roasted and cut into ½-inch strips
½	teaspoon red chile peppers, dried and chopped		1	tablespoon oregano
3	pounds pear tomatoes, diced		2	teaspoons salt
1	cup fresh parsley, minced		1	teaspoon pepper, coarse grind
			½	cup olive oil

Garlic Cream Sauce Ingredients

¼	pound butter		2	teaspoons salt
2	tablespoons fresh garlic, minced		1	teaspoon pepper
1	quart whipping cream			

Additional Ingredients

3	cups Parmesan cheese		1	pound lasagna noodles, cooked

For the Garlic Cream Sauce

MELT butter over medium-high heat in medium saucepan. Add garlic and simmer 2-3 minutes.

ADD cream, salt and pepper and simmer on low heat until sauce is reduced by one-third.

REMOVE from heat and cool in refrigerator until needed.

To make the Meat Sauce

ROAST and peel red peppers, then cut into ¼-inch strips.

PREHEAT large braising pan over medium-high heat.

WHEN pan is hot, add sausage and ground beef a little at a time so temperature doesn't drop rapidly. Meat should sizzle and smoke. Let meat brown on one side, then stir. Meat should be cooked to medium rare. Drain off excess fat.

ADD garlic, chile pepper, tomatoes, red pepper, parsley, oregano, salt and pepper. Simmer uncovered about 30 minutes until flavors blend and sauce thickens.

STIR in olive oil to bind sauce. Let sauce cool while cooking noodles.

To Assemble Tagliatelle

COMBINE cream sauce and meat sauce In a large container.

BEGIN layering ingredients in a large casserole or cake pan: sauce, noodles, and Parmesan cheese—making sure to use all ingredients and ending with sauce as the last layer.

COVER pan with foil. Bake in 350°F oven for 1 hour.

REMOVE from oven, let rest at room temperature for 30 minutes to set.

Serves 6

The state capitol.

Helena, Montana in its Gold Rush days.

TWO-COURSE PIZZA DINNER FOR TWO

One Half of Pizza—Prosciutto & Artichoke with Four Wisconsin Cheeses
Other Half of Pizza—Wisconsin Brie with Apples and Toasted Pine Nuts

Ingredients

1	12-inch pizza crust
6	ounces pizza sauce
2	ounces Parma prosciutto, sliced ⅛ x ⅛ x 1 inch
2	ounces artichoke hearts, cut in ⅛-inch pieces
4	ounces of 4 cheese blends, grated (equal parts Wisconsin Cheddar, Wisconsin Muenster, Wisconsin Parmesan, Wisconsin Provolone)

½   cup apricot preserves

5   ounces Wisconsin Brie–sliced ⅛ inch

1   large Granny Smith apple-cored, ⅛-inch slices, halved

1   tablespoon toasted pine nuts

2   tablespoon cinnamon sugar

Procedure

PREHEAT oven to 375°F (convection) or 425°F (conventional).

SPREAD pizza sauce over half of crust; spread apricot preserves over the other half of crust.

ARRANGE prosciutto over the pizza sauce and top with the four cheese blend. Arrange the artichokes neatly on top of the cheese. (This is a two-sided pizza. Be careful during assembly to keep the appropriate ingredients on the appropriate half of the crust.) Lay the slices of brie over the apricot side of the crust and arrange the apples neatly over the brie.

SPRINKLE the pine nuts over the brie and apples. Sift the cinnamon sugar over the top of the apple/brie side.

BAKE in preheated oven for 10 minutes (conventional oven) or 10-12 minutes (convection oven).

ALLOW pizza to rest for 3-5 minutes before slicing.

Serves 2

Fly Fishers Inn

2629 Old U.S. Hwy. 91
Cascade, Montana

406-468-2529
fish@flyfishersinn.com
www.flyfishersinn.com

Open to fly-fishing guests daily

Open to the public, Friday and
Saturday at 7:00 pm

Call for Reservations and
Information

The Fly Fishers Inn is nestled in a scenic canyon on the Missouri River.

The Fly Fishers Inn

Rick and Lynne Pasquale, Owners
Lynne Pasquale, Chef

Little did Lewis and Clark realize that the path of their trek in 1805 would eventually be viewed from a fly-fishing lodge complete with gourmet dining. Nestled in the Missouri Canyon, Fly Fishers Inn offers you comfort and convenience in a country setting. Overlooking the river at the foot of Mountain Palace Rock, the lodge houses the kitchen and dining room. The guest rooms are in a separate building, which was built in 1991 when the Pasquales purchased the property.

The original concept was to have a fly-fishing lodge serving unique meals to accommodate their fishing clients. It was an opportunity for Chef Lynne and Angler Rick to work together again.

The quality of the fishing on the Missouri River led the Pasquales to move from the East to Montana in 1981. It was never their intention to have the Inn. They started an outfitting business in 1985 operating out of Great Falls. The number of clients fishing the Missouri increased each year, until they saw a need for a location to lodge and feed their clients—and what better place than on the Missouri in the heart of fantastic fishing.

After a number of executive retreats were held at the Inn, Great Falls and Helena residents soon discovered the culinary ability of Lynne Pasquale. The Pasquales agreed to open the Inn for dinner to local gourmets on a reservation basis from April to December.

The pris-fixe, five course menus are published about every six weeks for the Friday and Saturday seating. With the current emphasis on healthy eating, the challenge has been to keep uniqueness, taste, and flavor while reducing the unhealthy ingredients. But don't look for this in Lynne's desserts.

The building that houses the lodge was originally built in 1936 when the "new" road between Helena and Great Falls was funded as part of the Depression economic recovery program. The business was a typical Montana roadside restaurant/bar that catered to those traveling between cities. It also served as an after church meeting place where families met and a spot where fishermen would stop to have something to eat or drink. When the Interstate was built in the late 1960s the building was bypassed and business declined.

Things have changed a lot since then. Lynne Pasquale's recipes and culinary skills have been published in a number of national magazines, including *Sunset* and *Town and Country*, as well as in her cookbook, *There's A Fly in My Soup*.

Tarragon Pea Soup

Can be served hot or cold

Ingredients

4	tablespoons unsalted butter
1	large onion (21-ounce), coarsely chopped
4	large garlic cloves, minced
6	cups chicken stock or broth
1	pound Idaho potatoes, peeled and quartered

1 ¾	pounds frozen sweet peas
½	teaspoon freshly ground black pepper
⅓	teaspoon cayenne pepper
2	tablespoons dried tarragon or 4 tablespoons fresh tarragon

Preparation

MELT the butter in a heavy saucepan over low heat. Add the onion and garlic, and cook gently until wilted and translucent, about 10 minutes. Add the stock or broth and potatoes; bring to a boil. Reduce the heat and cook until the potatoes are just tender, about 15 minutes. Remove the soup from the heat, let cool for about 10 minutes. Add the peas, cayenne and black pepper, and tarragon. Process the soup in batches in a food processor or blender until smooth. Add more chicken broth if needed or desired. Pour the soup through a strainer to remove any pieces of skin.

WHEN reheating the soup, don't overcook or your green pea soup will turn a khaki color. Reheat just before serving.

Makes about 9 cups of soup

POTATO FENNEL SOUP
Can be served hot or cold

Ingredients

3	large fennel bulbs, diced (reserve leaves for garnish)
1	large onion (about 21 oz. wt.), diced
2	tablespoons unsalted butter
2	medium russet baking potatoes (about a pound total weight)

2 ¾   cups chicken broth

1 ½   cups whipping cream

⅓   cup Sambucca or Anisette (anise-flavored liqueur)

Preparation

IN A LARGE heavy saucepan, cook diced fennel and onion in butter over moderate heat, stirring, until softened, about 10 minutes. Peel and cube potatoes. Add potatoes and broth to fennel mixture and simmer, covered, until potatoes are just tender, about 20 minutes. In a blender or food processor, purée mixture in batches until smooth and return to saucepan. Stir in whipping cream, Sambucca or Anisette, salt and pepper to taste and simmer soup, stirring occasionally, until heated through. Do not boil. Garnish soup with reserved fennel leaves.

Makes 6 cups of soup

PORK TENDERLOIN WITH PLUM SAUCE

Ingredients

2 14-ounce pork tenderloins	1 17-ounce can purple plums (including juice)
⅓ cup ruby port wine	1 tablespoon finely snipped fresh rosemary
½ teaspoon sugar	1½ teaspoons cornstarch
⅛ teaspoon salt	1 fresh purple plum, sliced into 12 thin slices
1 tablespoon water	

Preparation

PREHEAT oven to 350°F.

ROAST pork tenderloin uncovered on a rack in a shallow roasting pan. Insert meat thermometer. Roast uncovered in a 350°F oven for 25-35 minutes or until the thermometer registers 145°-155°F.

MEANWHILE, in a medium saucepan combine juice from can of purple plums (save canned plum fruit for garnish or for later use), port wine, rosemary, sugar, and salt. Bring to boil, simmer until reduced to about ½ cup. Stir together water and cornstarch. Stir cornstarch mixture into reduced wine and plum juice. Cook and stir until thickened and bubbly. If it is too thick, add a little more port wine to thin. Slice each roasted pork tenderloin diagonally into about 8 slices (giving each person 4 slices). Arrange 4 slices on each serving plate. Spoon a portion of the sauce onto sliced pork on each plate and garnish with 3 slices of fresh plum.

Serves 4

SEA BASS WITH MACADEMIA NUT CRUST
with Raspberry Butter Sauce

This is Lynne's signature dish. We started to prepare this in 1993 before sea bass became so popular. All of our seafood is flown in fresh from our seafood distributor, a dedicated fly fisherman who visits us regularly. All the fish products he sends are outstanding.

Ingredients

12	8-ounce sea bass filets, about 1-inch thick	1	cup melted, unsalted butter
1	cup fresh lime juice		

For the Crust

1	cup Panko bread crumbs	1	tablespoon minced fresh cilantro
½	cup chopped macadamia nuts	½	teaspoon salt (or more to taste)

For the Raspberry Butter Sauce

¼	cup minced shallots	½	cup raspberry vinegar
2	egg yolks	1	cup unsalted butter, melted

Preparation

PREHEAT oven to 350°F.

IN A food processor with the blade attachment, combine the Panko, chopped macadamia nuts, cilantro, and salt. Process until well-combined. Mixture should turn a very pale green color. You can taste the topping at this point and add more salt or cilantro if desired. Add cilantro by the sprig and add salt by the ¼ teaspoon until it is to your taste. Set mixture aside.

MARINATE sea bass filets in lime juice (add enough water to lime juice so fish filets are completely covered) for about an hour. Remove filets from lime juice/water marinade, pat dry, dip each filet into the melted butter and place on a greased cookie sheet or flat tray with about 1-inch sides. Add a little of the remaining melted butter to the Panko/macadamia nut mix and stir with a fork. Mixture should just stick together if you pick some up and squeeze it together with your fingers. It should not be gummy or very moist. Pat this mixture on top of each filet in a thin coating.

To Prepare Raspberry Butter Sauce

PUT SHALLOTS and raspberry vinegar in a small saucepan and bring to a simmer over low heat. Simmer until vinegar/shallot mixture is reduced to about ½ cup. Pour this mixture into a blender. Bring 1 cup melted unsalted butter to a simmer over medium heat. When the butter is bubbling, add the egg yolks to the blender with the vinegar mix and immediately turn the blender to a medium speed. (You'll have to keep the top on at first to avoid splashing.) With blender running, slowly remove top and begin to pour in the hot unsalted butter in a slow thin stream. This will create the emulsion that will be the raspberry butter sauce. When all the butter is incorporated into the egg yolks and vinegar, turn the blender off and scrape sauce into a small saucepan. This will keep (with a lid on) at room temperature for about 2-3 hours. You cannot heat it or it will separate. You can warm it slightly over simmering water (double boiler) until it is just warm, whisking constantly.

To Bake Fish

SLIDE tray with fish filets into preheated oven for approximately 15-20 minutes (or 17 minutes in a convection oven) until fish is slightly opaque in the center. (If a sharp knife will slide into the center of the filet with no resistance, the fish is done.) Do not overcook.

SERVE with a tablespoon of Raspberry Butter Sauce over top of fish. You can serve extra sauce in a dish for those who would like more.

Serves 6

There's some great fishing on the Missouri River.

LINGUINE WITH GARLIC, RAISINS, & PINE NUTS

Ingredients

¼ cup extra virgin olive oil

4 large cloves garlic, peeled,
   plus 2 cloves, minced

½ cup golden raisins

½ cup dark raisins

½ cup pine nuts

¼ teaspoon crushed red pepper flakes

12 ounces dried linguine pasta

    Salt and fresh ground pepper to taste

    Parmesan cheese, freshly grated for
    serving

⅓ cup parsley, chopped

    Croutons

Preparation

HEAT the olive oil in a large heavy skillet over low heat. Add the whole garlic cloves and cook until they begin to color, about 10 minutes. Remove from the heat and discard the garlic cloves. Set the skillet with oil aside. Just before serving, bring a large pot of salted water to a boil. Add pasta and cook until just tender. Drain well, and place in pasta serving pot.

MEANWHILE, as the pasta is cooking, add the minced garlic, raisins, pine nuts, and red pepper flakes to the reserved skillet with oil and place over low heat. Cook until the garlic just begins to brown, 8 to 10 minutes. Do not let it burn. Add the mixture to the hot pasta, and toss. Season with salt and pepper. Serve immediately with a bowl of freshly grated Parmesan; sprinkle parsley and a few croutons over the top of the pasta as a garnish.

Serves 6

TRIPLE OLIVE SAUCE
Served over Pasta

Ingredients

2   tablespoons olive oil

⅓   cup sliced pitted black olives

1   (7-ounce) red onion, diced

⅓   cup sliced, pitted green olives

3   garlic cloves, minced

⅓   cup sliced, pitted Kalamata olives

¾   tablespoons dried oregano

½   cup grated Parmesan cheese

¼   teaspoon dried crushed red pepper

1   14½-ounce can diced tomatoes and juice

1   pounds Roma tomatoes, seeded and diced

12 ounces pasta

Preparation

HEAT oil in heavy Dutch oven over medium-high heat. Add chopped onion, garlic, oregano, and crushed red pepper and sauté until onion is translucent (about 3-5 minutes). Add canned diced tomatoes, Roma tomatoes, and all olives. Simmer sauce for about 5-8 minutes.

COOK pasta (of your choice) in boiling salted water. Add a little sauce and juices to cooked and drained pasta. Toss to moisten pasta thoroughly. Divide pasta among serving plates, put about a half-cup of sauce on top of pasta and generously top with grated Parmesan.

Serves 6

CHOCOLATE ESPRESSO TORTE
with Chocolate Glaze

Ingredients for the Torte

12 ounces semi-sweet chocolate, coarsely chopped

1 pound unsalted butter (4 sticks)

1 cup espresso coffee (liquid)

1 cup dark brown sugar

8 eggs, slightly beaten
  Parchment or waxed paper

Ingredients for the Chocolate Glaze

8 ounces semi-sweet chocolate, chopped

12 tablespoon unsalted butter, cut into tablespoons

5 teaspoons water

1 tablespoon light corn syrup

8 ounces white chocolate for garnish

Ingredients for the Garnish

Chocolate leaves, chocolate curls, or white chocolate melted and striped over each piece

To Prepare the Torte

PREHEAT oven to 325°F (convection) or 350°F (conventional).

TRACE and cut out waxed or parchment paper to fit the bottom of a 9-inch springform pan. Grease bottom of the springform pan and line with parchment or waxed paper, then grease the sides and the waxed-paper bottom. In a saucepan, bring butter, espresso, and sugar to a boil. Keep stirring until sugar dissolves. Place 12 ounces of chopped chocolate into a bowl. Pour butter mixture into the chopped chocolate. Whisk until chocolate is melted and mixture is smooth. Keep whisking as you very, very slowly pour eggs into chocolate mixture. Now, pour the batter into prepared springform pan. Place springform pan in a roasting pan. Add boiling water to roasting pan until water comes halfway up sides of roasting pan. Bake 1 hour (45 minutes convection). Place on cooling rack. Run thin-bladed knife around inside of pan to loosen torte. Cool, then chill overnight.

The Next Day: Assembly and Glaze

REMOVE sides from springform pan. Cut a piece of cardboard to fit torte or place tart on a metal tart pan bottom (or any flat tray with no sides) to apply glaze. (Glaze will run onto metal tray but will set up in refrigerator and can be cut away before serving.) Set cardboard or tray on top of torte. Invert torte. Place on pedestal (if you have one). Slide knife between pan bottom and paper to release. Press lightly on cake to smooth out any uneven spots. Combine all glaze ingredients in a bowl. Microwave at 50 percent power for 3 minutes. Stop and stir after each minute (or set in a double boiler over pot of simmering water and stir until glaze becomes very smooth). Whisk glaze until it becomes very smooth. This is important when you start pouring it over the cake. Pour warm glaze over torte, letting it coat sides.

POUR rather fast because that cold torte makes the glaze set up fast. Use a knife to lightly touch up only the uncoated areas. Don't touch anything else or you'll get marks. Let glaze set up in the refrigerator for about 1 hour before serving. Cut into 18 pieces. It's very rich so a small piece is plenty. Garnish with chocolate curls, chocolate leaves, or melt white chocolate, put it in a small Ziplock bag, cut off one corner, and pour thin stripes of melted white chocolate over each piece in crisscross pattern. Can also be garnished with raspberry purée and fresh raspberries.

Serves 14–18

Ginger Tart with Raspberry Sauce

This one is a sleeper. We never thought so many of our guests would like this tart.

Dough

1 cup all-purpose flour	½ cup (1 stick) chilled unsalted butter, cut into pieces
⅓ cup sugar	
¼ teaspoon salt	5 tablespoons cold water

Filling

1½ cups packed golden brown sugar	1 tablespoon grated peeled fresh ginger
¼ cup (½ stick) unsalted butter	1½ cups sliced almonds
3 tablespoons whipping cream	4 large egg yolks
1 tablespoon all purpose flour	

For Dough

PREHEAT oven to 375°F.

COMBINE flour, sugar, and salt in processor. Add butter, cut in using on/off pulses until mixture resembles coarse meal. Add water, a little at a time, and pulse just until moist clumps form. Knead dough gently until smooth. Cover; chill 20 minutes. Roll out dough on floured surface to 13-inch round. Fit into a 10-inch diameter tart pan with removable bottom. Trim edges. Chill until firm, about 30 minutes. Line dough with foil. Fill with pie weights or dried beans. Bake in oven until crust sets, about 8-15 minutes. Remove weights and foil. Bake crust until pale golden, about 8-20 minutes longer (checking often). Transfer to rack and cool. Reduce oven temperature to 250°F (convection) or 300°F (conventional) oven.

For Filling

COMBINE brown sugar, butter, whipping cream, all-purpose flour, and grated ginger in heavy large skillet. Stir over low heat until sugar dissolves, about 5 minutes. Remove from heat; stir in nuts. Cool slightly. Add yolks and stir to combine thoroughly. Pour filling into prebaked crust and bake until filling looks dry and crusty and center is softly set, about 20-30 minutes. Increase oven temperature to 300°F (convection) or 325°F (conventional) oven. Continue baking until center is set, about 10 to 15 minutes longer. Transfer to rack; cool completely. Can be made one day ahead. Cover and chill. Bring to room temperature before continuing.

For the Raspberry Sauce

ONE 12-ounce bag frozen raspberries, thawed and puréed in blender or food processor. Strain to remove seeds. Add sugar to taste. Put into a clean ketchup squeeze bottle and squeeze a design on dessert plates. Put slice of tart on top of design. Serve with whipped cream. Garnish with Raspberry Sauce.

Serves 12

CULINARY SOURCES

CERTIFIED ORGANIC LAMB AND GRASS-FED
BEEF AS WELL AS WOOL PRODUCTS
THIRTEEN MILE LAMB & WOOL COMPANY
13000 Springhill Road, Belgrade, MT 59714
406-388-4945 Fax 406-388-1956
becky@lambandwool.com

SPECIALIZING IN WILD GAME & GOURMET
PANTRY ITEMS
VALLEY GAME & GOURMET
P.O. Box 2713
Salt Lake City, UT 84110
www.valleygame.com
1-800-521-2156 or 801-521-2345

FRESH & SMOKED PHEASANTS, CHUKAR PAR-
TRIDGE, QUAIL, DUCK, ALSO WILD RICE
OAKWOOD GAME FARMS
P.O. Box 274, Princeton, MN 55371
1-800-328-6647
www.oakgamefarm.com

ELK, BUFFALO, CARIBOU, ANTELOPE, RABBIT,
QUAIL, TURKEY, PHEASANTS, DUCKS, MUSH-
ROOMS, BERRIES
NATIVE GAME COMPANY
308 Walnut, Brighton, CO 80601
1-800-364-3007
www.nativegame.bigstep.com

BUFFALO, ELK, VENSION, WILD BOAR, RABBIT,
PHEASANT, QUAIL, DUCK, GOOSE; MUSH-
ROOMS, BERRIES, AND FOIE GRAS
PRAIRIE HARVEST SPECIALTY FOODS
P.O. Box 1013, Spearfish, SD 57783
www.prairieharvest.com

ANTELOPE, VENSION, WILD BOAR
BROKEN ARROW RANCH
P.O. Box 530, Ingram, TX 78025
1-800-962-4263
www.brokenarrowranch.com

TRUFFLES
THE TRUFFLE MARKET
P.O. Box 4234, Gettysburg, PA 17325
1-800-822-4003
www.trufflemarket.com

MUSHROOMS AND TRUFFLE OILS
GOURMET MUSHROOM PRODUCTS
P.O. Box 515 IP, Graton, CA 9544
1-800-789-9121
www.gmushrooms.com

COMPLETE SELECTION OF CAVIAR -
FOREIGN AND DOMESTIC
CAVIAR DIRECT
1-800-650-2828
www.cavier-direct.com
email cavier@caviar-direct.com

COMPLETE SELECTION OF FRESH SEAFOOD,
TRUFFLES AND TOBIKKO CAVIAR
THE FRESHEST SEAFOOD
1111 NW 45st Suite B, Seattle, WA 98107
1-877-706-4022
www.seafoodfoodsuperstore.com
email info@simplyseafood.com

COMPLETE SELECTION OF SPICES
PENZEYS SPICES
19300 West Janacek Court
P.O. Box 924, Brookfield, WI 53308
1-800-741-7787
www.penzeys.com

HUCKLEBERRY JAMS, SYRUPS, SAUCES
THE HUCKLEBERRY PEOPLE
1021 Waverly Street, Missoula, MT 59802
1-800-735-6462
www.huckleberrypeople.com

CHOCOLATE OBAN WAFERS, CANDIES
THE CANDY WAREHOUSE
5314 Third Street, Irwindale, CA 91706
626-480-0899 Fax: 626-480-0818
www.candywarehouse.com

FAST DELIVERY FOR SPECIALTY FOODS
(PREPARED CANNOLI SHELLS, PASTAS, ETC.)
AND KITCHEN TOOLS
THE NEXT DAY GOURMET
www.nextdaygourmet.com

THE DEFINITIVE SOURCE FOR CULINARY
QUESTIONS, DEFINITIONS AND RECIPES
www.epicurious.com

GLOSSARY

al dente
Used to describe pasta or other food that is cooked only until it offers a slight resistance when bitten into, but which is not overcooked.

aioli
A mayonnaise strongly seasoned with garlic or other seasoning, usually served as an accompaniment for fish, meats, and vegetables.

andouille
Spicy, heavily-smoked sausage.

bain-marie
A utensil used to gently cook sauces and soups so that they do not come to a boil. Similar to a double boiler if used on stovetop. In the oven, it can be a roasting pan filled with water in which the food container is placed.

béarnaise sauce
A classic French sauce made with vinegar, wine, tarragon, and shallots that have been reduced, finished with egg yolks and butter.

bake in hot water bath
See bain-marie above. In baking, you would put a shallow pan filled with a couple of inches of warm water in the oven and set your filled baking pan inside.

butterfly
To split food (such as shrimp or chicken breast) down the middle, but not completely through. The breast is opened to cook, resembling a butterfly.

capers
The flower bud of a bush native to the Mediterranean and parts of Asia. The small buds are picked, sun-dried, and then pickled in a vinegar brine.

chèvre cheese
French for "goat," chèvre is a pure white goat's-milk cheese with a tart flavor.

caul fat
The thin fat-laced membrane covering an animal's stomach.

chiffonade
A method similar to julienne, but refers mainly to cutting lettuce, endive, or herbs into thin, even strips.

chitterlings
Stomach lining (pork, beef, sheep).

chipotle
A dried, smoked, Jalepino. Has a sweet, almost chocolatey flavor.

chorizo
A spicy, coarsely ground pork sausage flavored with chile powder and garlic, usually in Mexican dishes.

clarified
Refers to a process of clearing a cloudy substance, such as in stocks or wines. Also refers to the process of melting unsalted butter until the foam rises. After skimming the foam off, the yellow liquid left can be heated to a much higher temperature than regular butter.

confectioners' sugar
Powdered sugar.

court bullion
A poaching liquid usually made up of vegetables, water, herbs and wine or vinegar.

crème anglaise
A cooked mixture of cream, sugar, egg yolks, and usually vanilla for flavoring. Often used as part of a dessert recipe.

crostini
Small, thin slices of toasted bread, usually brushed with olive oil. Means "little toasts" in Italian.

crème fraîche
A thick, velvety cream that can be boiled without curdling. Hard to find commercially and very expensive, but can be made simply by stirring well, 1 cup whipping cream and 2 tablespoons buttermilk in a glass container. Cover and let stand at room temperature (about 70°F) until thick (8-24 hours). Refrigerate up to 10 days.

de-bearding
To pull the threads towards the hinge of the mussel and tear out.

demi-glace	A rich brown sauce (usually meat stock) combined with Madiera or sherry and slowly cooked until it's reduced by half to a thick glaze.
deglaze	After food has been browned and fat removed, add a little wine or water to the skillet to loosen browned bits on the bottom to make a sauce.
demi-sec	In cooking, it refers to reducing by half. In wine, it refers to the level of sweetness.
dore	Golden brown.
foie gras	The term generally used for goose liver.
frenched	To trim fat or bone from a cut of meat.
gazpacho	A cold, summertime vegetable soup.
gratinée	To brown (usually crumbs and butter) under a broiler or with a torch.
gremulata	A garnish made of minced parsley, lemon peel, and garlic to add a fresh, sprightly flavor.
gumbo filé	Powdered, dried leaves of the sassafras tree, generally used in Creole cooking.
julienne	A method of cutting vegetables into thin strips, usually about 1 inch by $\frac{1}{16}$ inch.
kosher salt	An additive-free coarse-grained salt used in the preparation of meat by gourmet cooks who prefer its texture and flavor.
mascarpone	An Italian cream cheese; double- to triple-rich and buttery.
meunière	Lightly dusting a meat or fish in flour and sauteeing in butter, usually with lemon juice sprinkled on top.
morel mushroom	An edible wild mushroom belonging to the same fungus species as the truffle.
mirin	A sweet, rice wine used in cooking to sweeten meat or fish dishes.
napoleon	A dish made with a variety of layers, usually a dessert.
nappe	Usually referring to a coating, such as a sauce that has thickened enough to coat a spoon.
Oban wafers	A type of chocolate wafer. (See Culinary Sources.)
paella	A Spanish rice dish with a variety of meats or shellfish, or vegetables (garlic, onions, peas, artichoke hearts, and tomatoes) usually flavored with saffron.
pancetta	A slightly salty Italian bacon cured with salt and spices, but not smoked.
Panko	Coarse bread crumbs (Japanese) used for coating fried foods. Create a deliciously crunchy outer crust. Available in supermarkets.
prosciutto	Italian word for ham; seasoned, salt-cured and air-dried, but not smoked.
purée	To grind or mash food until it's completely smooth, by using a food processor, a blender, or by forcing the food through a sieve.
ragout	A stew made of meats or vegetables, well-seasoned and thickened.
ramekin	An individual earthenware baking dish (3 to 4 inches in diameter) that resembles a miniature soufflé dish.

reduce (reduction)	To boil a liquid rapidly (stock, wine, or a sauce mixture) until the volume reduces by evaporation, thickening the consistency and intensifying the flavor.
render	To convert or melt down fat by slow heating.
ribbon stage	The stage in a recipe when the ingredients you are beating (usually egg yolks and sugar) thicken enough to flow from your whisk or spoon in a continuous ribbon.
roux	A mixture of equal parts flour and butter used to thicken sauces. Cooking different lengths of time results in different flavors and colors.
sauté	To quickly cook food over direct heat in a small amount of hot oil.
shallot	Member of the onion family.
steep	To soak dry ingredients (leaves, coffee, herbs, spices, etc.) in liquid (usually hot) until the flavor is infused into the liquid.
sushi rice	A round-grained rice that becomes slightly sticky when cooked, so that it can be mixed with other ingredients and shaped in a roll.
sweat	To cook vegetables slowly in their own juices. A little butter or oil is often used to start the process, and then the mixture is covered to let the moisture in the vegetables release.
tapenade	A spread or condiment, usually consisting of capers, olives, anchovies mashed with olive oil.
tartare	Often refers to a raw meat dish.
tartar sauce	A sauce usually served with fish, and consisting of mayonnaise, capers, onion, olives and pickles.
temper	Most often refers to slightly warming beaten eggs, by rapidly stirring a little of the hot ingredients into them, before adding them to the hot mixture so that they will combine without solidifying.
tomato stricia	Commercially-available tomatoes cut in strips and packed in a puree.
Tobikko	Caviar, flying fish roe.
tripe	Most commonly, the lining of the beef stomach, although it could be pork or sheep. Usually fairly tough and requires longer cooking periods.
truffle	A fungus that is cultivated primarily in France and Italy today. It is grown underneath the ground, usually at the base of certain trees such as oak and chestnut. Highly prized for its earthy, aromatic nature.
truffle oil	Truffle oil is created when truffles are soaked in olive oil.
tuile	A flavored thin, crisp cookie that is usually curved.
U-15 shrimp	Pertains to the size of the shrimp; the number following the U denotes the number of shrimp per pound (approximately).
wilted spinach /lettuce	Using a steam process to wilt spinach or lettuce, or drizzling a hot liquid or bacon grease over the vegetables to cause them to wilt.
zest	The brightly colored outermost skin layer of citrus fruit, removed with a zester, grater, or knife.

ABOUT THE PUBLISHERS

Chuck and Blanche started Wilderness Adventures Press, Inc. in 1993, publishing outdoor and sporting books. Along with hunting and fishing, they love fine dining, good wines, and traveling. They have always been able to "sniff out" the most outstanding and interesting restaurants in any city they visit.

On weekends, they experiment in the kitchen, cooking a variety of fish and meats, as well as preparing the harvest from their time in the field. This love of cooking has resulted in a large library of cookbooks, and has inspired them to create a series of cookbooks based on their love of travel and fine dining.

Chuck and Blanche make their home in Gallatin Gateway, Montana, along with their four German wirehaired pointers.

PHOTO COPYRIGHTS/CREDITS

Cover, left to right across: ©Art Today (*pheasant*); ©the Mint Bar and Cafe (*exterior sign*); ©Chuck Robbins (Madison River); ©Art Today (*Grinnell Glacier*), ©Continental Divide Restaurant (*Broiled Foie Gras*), ©Potosi Hot Springs (*old hotel*), ©Lone Mountain Ranch (*dining room*), ©Erik Peterson (*Montana Cowboy*),©Triple Creek Ranch (*patio dining*), ©Triple Creek Ranch (*Rack of Lamb*), ©Grand Hotel-Kalispell (*historic photo*), ©Art Today (*bison*). **Back cover left to right across:** ©Blanche and Chuck Johnson (*Potosi Hot Springs*), ©Buck's T-4 (*Big Sky*), ©Grand Union Hotel (*Fort Benton*), ©Gallatin River Lodge (*Bozeman*), ©Lone Mountain Ranch (*Big Sky*), ©John Bozeman's Bistro (*the chefs*) i: ©Gallatin County Historical Society (*picnic*) iii: ©Travel Montana, Donnie Sexton (*bing cherries*). iv: ©Marcia Rueter Leritz (*mushrooms*). v: ©Marcia Rueter Leritz (*Bridger Mountains*). vi: ©Marcia Rueter Leritz (*fairy slipper*). vii: ©*Gallatin County Historical Society*. vii: ©Gallatin County Historical Society (*Gallatin River and Bozeman*). viii: ©Gallatin County Historical Society (*Gallatin River and pack string*). xii: ©Wilderness Adventures Press (*map*). xiv-left: ©Gallatin County Historical Society. xiv-right: ©Marcia Rueter Leritz. 1, 2: ©Enzo Mediterranean Bistro. 5: ©Gallatin County Historical Society (steamboat). 6: ©Art Today7, 8, 10: ©Walkers Grill. 12: ©Marcia Rueter Leritz (*Bridger Mountains*).13, 14, 15:©Pollard Hotel. 19, 20, 21, 25-right:©Chico Hot Springs Resort. 20-right, 25-left: ©Gallatin County Historical Society. 29: ©Marcia Rueter Leritz. 30-top, bottom right: ©Boodles. 30-bottom left, 33: ©Gallatin County Historical Society. 35: ©Marcia Rueter Leritz. 36, **top and bottom left**, 37, 38: ©John Bozeman's Bistro. 36-bottom right:©Gallatin County Historical Society. 38: ©John Bozeman's Bistro. 39, 40: ©Gallatin River Lodge. 42: ©Gallatin County Historical Society. 43, 44: ©Mint Bar & Cafe. 49, 50, 51: ©Bucks T-4 Lodge. 57, 58, 62: ©Lone Mountain Ranch. 63, 64, 65: ©The Timbers at Moonlight Lodge. 69, 70, 71-left, 72: ©320 Guest Ranch. 71-right, 74: ©Gallatin County Historical Society. 75: ©Wilderness Adventures Press, Inc. 76: ©Healing Waters Lodge. 81, 82-bottom left and right: © 2002 Bearfeather Studio/Ken Hall. 82-top, 85: ©Continental Divide Restaurant. 87, 88, 89-right: ©Blanche and Chuck Johnson. 89-left: ©Potosi Hot Springs. 96-left: ©Blanche and Chuck Johnson.96-right: ©Potosi Hot Springs. 97: ©Marcia Rueter Leritz (*Big Hole River*). 98, 102: ©Jackson Hot Springs Lodge. 106: ©Gallatin County Historical Society. 107, 108, 109, 110: ©Triple Creek Ranch. 115: ©Donnie Sexton/Travel Montana. 116: ©The Bridge Bistro. 116-bottom left: ©Michael Hewston, www.screensavers.com. 119, 120,122: ©Red Bird Restaurant. 124: ©Art Today. 125, 126, 127, 128, 129, 130: ©Double Arrow Resort. 131, 132-top: ©La Provence Restaurant. 132-bottom, 133, 136: ©Ted Habarth.137: ©Michael Hewston, www.screensavers.com.138, 139-right: ©Kalispell Grand Hotel. 139-left: ©Michael Hewston, www.screensavers.com. 144: ©Donnie Sexton/Travel Montana. 145: ©Marcia Leritz. 146-top, bottom right: ©Cafe Max. 146-bottom left: ©Michael Hewston, www.screensavers.com. 150: ©Art Today. 151: ©Art Today. 152, 153: ©Pollo Grill. 156: ©Art Today. 158: ©Marcia Rueter Leritz.159, 160, 162: ©Tupelo Grille & Wine Bar. 163, 164, 165: ©Whitefish Lake Golf Club. 168: ©Art Today. 169, 170, 171: St. Mary Lodge. 174: ©Donnie Sexton/Travel Montana. 177: ©Donnie Sexton/Travel Montana (*Missouri River*). 178: ©Great Falls Chamber of Commerce. 182: ©Marcia Rueter Leritz (*Missouri River at Fort Benton*).183, 184, 185, 187: ©Grand Union Hotel. 189: ©Donnie Sexton/Travel Montana. 190: ©Jen Tzenis. 190-bottom left: ©Marcia Rueter Leritz. 193-top: ©Donnie Sexton/Travel Montana.193-bottom: ©Gallatin County Historical Society. 195, 196, 197, 198, 199, 201: ©Fly Fishers Inn

INDEX